Incurable!

*What to Do When
God Says It's Over*

PAUL
SCHWANKE

CONTENTS

"HIS WOUND IS mortal. It is impossible for him to recover."[1]

11 words staggered an entire nation. A 23 year old doctor, Charles Leale, had gazed into the dull pupils of President Abraham Lincoln, and recognized there was no brain function. Heroic efforts to save the President's life would last through that fateful night, but nine hours later, he would gasp his final breath, and, in the words of the Secretary of War, Edwin Stanton, Mr. Lincoln would "belong to the ages".

The celebration of a nation rejoicing over an ended Civil War abruptly shifted to immense mourning. A gamut of emotion filled the streets of Washington D.C., rapidly exploding through the entire country. A wife, a son, friends, and citizens were overcome with indescribable grief.

What horrifying words; "His wound is mortal."

Some 2560 years earlier, a prophet of God heard a similar diagnosis. The prophet was named Micah. The speaker was the Great Physician, Almighty God. The words were directed to the nations of Israel and Judah. It sounded like this:

"Her wound is incurable" (Micah 1:9).

The pronouncement overwhelmed Micah. How could he possibly be prepared for such words? All Bible preachers, irrespective of hopeless circumstances, of helpless complications, of heartbreaking catastrophes, have an unwavering confidence that there is always a way with God. A thief on a cross can be saved. A prodigal son can come home. A desperate woman can come to the well. So long as a heart is beating, there remains an abiding hope that the marvelous mercy of God will conquer the most impossible situation.

"Her wound is incurable".

What a final message. A patient is told by a doctor, "We have done our best, but there is no cure for the cancer. There is no pill. There is no procedure." They are sent home to die. The clock is about to strike midnight, and there is nothing that anyone can do about it. "Incurable" is a lonely word, a demoralizing word, a terrifying word.

God had just told Micah there was no fix for Israel, his relatives living to the north. That wound had "come unto Judah", as Micah and his people were but months behind their backsliding brothers. It was time to push the panic button.

"Her wound is incurable"

CHAPTER ONE

AN OFFER RESCINDED

SOME 25 MILES southwest of Jerusalem was a little village called Moresh. It would be hard to imagine that such an inconspicuous, insignificant place could ever house a mighty man of God, yet we humans are continually reminded that "God hath chosen the foolish things of the world to confound the wise; and God hath chosen the weak things of the world to confound the things which are mighty" (1 Corinthians 1:27). From those dusty streets came "Micah the Morasthite".

It was appropriate that such a humble town produce a humble preacher from a humble family. Prophets like Jeremiah, Ezekiel, Jonah, and Hosea are known by their father's name, but not Micah. The only thing we know about his dad is that he gave his son a godly name.

Good preachers develop distinct styles, and Micah developed a skill in preaching names. He would preach about city names. He would preach about God's name. He even found a way to preach on his own name. "Micah" means "who is like the Lord", and before this powerful book of the Bible concludes, the man of God preaches these words:

"Who is a God like unto thee, that pardoneth iniquity, and passeth by the transgression of the remnant of his heritage" (Micah 7:18)?

As God prepared Micah to travel to the villages and smaller cities that dotted the map of Judah, He also readied a man named Isaiah to work in the capital of Jerusalem. God had His man to work with the common folk, and God had His man to work with the 'big-city' folk. We often limit our thinking to our group, our school, our fellowship, yet God is well able to use His "babes and sucklings" (Psalms 8:2). It is His work, not ours.

As Isaiah begins his prophecy, he steps into the courtroom of the skies. The trial of the ages is unfolding, and the man of God has been ushered into the gallery as a witness. The gavel has come down, and the trial is ready to commence:

"Hear, O heavens, and give ear, O earth: for the Lord hath spoken" (Isaiah 1:2).

At the witness stand, Almighty God is ready to present His case. It would be hard to imagine, from a human point of view, a scenario more distressing than hearing the God of the Bible lay out a series of accusations. He knows "...my downsitting and mine uprising...(my) thoughts... my path...my lying down...my ways..." (Psalm 139:2-3). Every word ever spoken, every step ever taken, every thought ever visualized, all are heard and seen and known by God. He knows our actions, our motives, and our intent. He is not just an ideal witness, He is the consummate witness, and He is now presenting His dispute against His people.

"I have nourished and brought up children, and they have rebelled against me." It is a "...sinful nation, a people laden with iniquity". "They have forsaken the Lord, they have provoked the Holy One of Israel unto anger." "From the sole of the foot even unto the head there is no soundness in it; but wounds, and bruises, and putrifying sores."

The condition had deteriorated to the place where God called it "desolate", "overthrown", and "besieged". The nation had rebelled to the point where God named them the "rulers of Sodom" and the "people of Gomorrah". Even their religious sacrifices were "vain" and an "abomination", and they were so loaded with hypocrisy, that God said He actually hated their holidays ("appointed feasts") (Isaiah 1:2-14).

If a simple reading of Isaiah 1 in our present day causes us to tremble and fear, imagine the horror of Isaiah, as he sees and hears the charges God lays against the people. The summary of the litigation causes God to threaten them, "And when ye spread forth your hands, I will hide mine eyes from you: Yea, when ye make many prayers, I will not hear"(Isaiah 1:15). The charges are worse than imagined, and the penalty could not be more severe. For their sins and rebellion, God was going to judge them. He would not hear their cries, and He would not respond to their sorrow. The "wages of sin" were about to produce "death" (Romans 6:23), and the terror of God was going to fall upon the land.

Suddenly, the trial is interrupted with the plea bargain of the ages. No defendant so guilty has ever received such an offer. Condemned and doomed, the people of Jerusalem watch the wrath of God morph into the mercy of God, and a proposal bursting with the marvelous love of Heaven falls upon their ears:

"Come now, and let us reason together, saith the Lord: Though your sins be as scarlet, they shall be as white as snow; though they be red like crimson, they shall be as wool" (Isaiah 1:18).

Too good to be true! God is offering pardon and forgiveness to those who are "willing and obedient" (Isaiah 1:19). Mercy is great! Grace is free! 'Pardon there is multiplied to me!' How glorious is the goodness of God.

Now it is Micah's turn. He follows the steps of Isaiah into the hallowed courtroom of the skies, as the Lord GOD prepares to be the witness yet again. "Hear, all ye people; hearken, O earth, and all that therein is: and let the Lord God be witness against you, the Lord from his holy temple" (Micah 1:2). He sees God coming in mighty power, treading the high places of the earth. Those mountaintops were considered the residences of the gods, yet every step He takes leaves a crushed mountain, as useless as the wax dripping down the sides of a melted candle (Micah 1:4).

Though the first charges are leveled against Judah's brothers to the north, the people of Samaria, there could be no rest for the Micah and his people, for the sins that filled Israel had "come unto Judah" (Micah 1:9). Micah hears God promise to smash the graven images, to burn the harlots, and to make the idols desolate. Overwhelming words cascade from the trial as the people are warned yet again.

But this time, there is no plea bargain. This time, Heaven has no offer. Isaiah heard, "Come now, and let us reason together". Micah heard a different message.

"Her wound is incurable".

The Problem

"Righteousness exalteth a nation:
but sin is a reproach to any people."

(Proverbs 14:34)

CHAPTER TWO

WHEN IS ENOUGH ENOUGH?

STEPHEN SPIELBERG, Frank Lautenburg, Zsa Zsa Gabor, Sandy Koufax, Phyllis George, and Larry King are famous names in America. Through the years, their stories and exploits have filled our front pages, our sports pages, our political pages, and our entertainment pages. Yet, fame is not the only thing they have in common.

They were all ripped off by Bernie Madoff.

Federal investigators believe that his massive Ponzi scheme, the largest fraud in American history, may have been hatched as far back as the 70's. By the time Madoff was convicted in March of 2009, $65,000,000,000 (billion) was missing, and the infamous swindler was sentenced to 150 years behind bars.

Major corporations like J.P. Morgan and the New York Mets were caught up in scandal. Hypocritical Senators Chris Dodd and Charles Schumer scrambled to return campaign donations. Foundations and charities lost an incredible amount of money, banks and investment firms lost their clients' wealth, and pension funds were decimated.[2]

Yet, the most heart-breaking stories were of the people no one had ever heard of. Private investors had trusted Bernie Madoff with their retirement and financial future, and in a 'Wall Street minute', it was gone. Entire lives of hard work, saving, and discipline washed away into a New York sewer, victim of one man's greed.

It wasn't the first time.

The prophet Micah and his people had their brand of 'Madoff', reminding us that humans and their sins have not changed so much these past 25 centuries. The man of God thundered against the sin with these words:

"Woe to them that devise iniquity, and work evil upon their beds! When the morning is light, they practise it, because it is in the power of their hand. And they covet fields, and take them by violence; and houses, and take them away: So they oppress a man and his house, even a man and his heritage" (Micah 2:1-2).

Corrupt businessmen lay awake all night long, conjuring up schemes and strategies to separate people from their heritage, a Bible term referring to an inheritance or a property. Their 'devising' was an illegal abuse of power, an action taken against poor people, a plan they put in place as the morning dawned. In Micah's day, the morning was thought to be the hour of justice, the time of the day when kings would hold court. The night belonged to the evil, but the morning was expected to bring light to the darkness.

Not anymore.

Their covetousness and greed dominated their actions. When God told Joshua to divide the land of Israel, He wanted families to own their land forever (Leviticus 25:23-28). Such avaricious operators have no concern for God's Word. Their pompous attitude says, "Might is right. I want it and I will take it." Like Ahab of old, they spoil their own Naboths and his vineyard. They "covet", they "take", and they "oppress", caring nothing for ruined fortunes, futures, and families.

Scheming thieves laying awake all night always make a deadly error. They forget that while they are plotting their next move in the darkness, someone else is also alert. In the still of the night, they never imagine they are being watched. Someone is listening. Someone is observing. Someone knows.

"Behold, he that keepeth Israel shall neither slumber nor sleep" (Psalm 121:4).

The living God of the Bible had something to say!

"Therefore thus saith the LORD; Behold, against this family do I devise an evil, from which ye shall not remove your necks; neither shall ye go haughtily: for this time is evil" (Micah 2:3).

God promised He would do as He has done through the ages of time. He would punish them "according to the fruit of your doings" (Jeremiah 21:14). They had attacked families so God attacked their family. They had "devised" against the poor, so God "devised" against them. They had oppressed, so God put them in a yoke from which they would never shake loose. They were haughty, so God broke their pride. They spoiled the helpless, so God saw that they were spoiled. As they had divided up the fields of their victims, so God would divide their fields, and give them to the Assyrian warriors.

"Behold, the righteous shall be recompensed in the earth: much more the wicked and the sinner" (Proverbs 11:31).

God wasn't finished. He told them the day would come when they would be taunted. The Bible phrase, "doleful lamentation", poetically describes the "parable" their lives told. Their wicked wealth would become a distant memory, their ill-gotten gains would provide no pleasure, and as they were being led away captive by invading forces, no one would be left to cast lots, and divvy up the land as Joshua had done.

How different was Micah from modern day ministers! Perhaps one of the reasons business scandals rock America's core stems from the silence of preachers. Could it be that Kenneth Lay, the disgraced CEO of Enron, a symbol of greed and arrogance, received a pass because he was the son of a Baptist minister? Could it be that America's pulpits were silenced by his generous contributions? Could it be that too many preachers are simply puppets on the strings of those that finance their multi-million dollar businesses?[3]

The 'Wall Street' of Micah's day was corrupt, greedy, and abusive, but the problem did not stop at the luxurious offices of pompous executives. The crookedness had also found its way to their 'Walmart.'

It was impossible to buy one's daily food without dealing with the pilfering. The markets were full of salespeople that would use "...scant measure(s)...wicked balance(s)...bag(s) of deceitful weights" (Micah 6:10-11). One can hear the shyster say, "Put your grain in my bushel. Lay your fruit on my scale. Let me weigh your vegetables." But the bushel was not full size. The scale would have a slightly twisted crossbow unseen by the human eye. The counter-weights would be inaccurate.

The common man didn't have a chance. He was robbed of his large bills and his small coins. No one could be trusted. No one was honest. The dirty cancer of greed filtered to every level of society, and nothing was more important than 'one more dollar'. If it took "...violence...lies...(or) deceit" (Micah 6:12), what did it matter? Exploitation had become their way of life - after all, everyone did it.

But God had something to say. "Therefore also will I make thee sick in smiting thee, In making thee desolate because of thy sins" (Micah 6:13). They may have laughed all the way to the bank, but God was not laughing in the courtroom of the skies. He had a four word commentary for them.

"Her wound is incurable".

The famous Russian writer, Leo Tolstoy, once wrote a story about a successful peasant farmer who was not satisfied with his lot. He wanted more of everything.

One day he received a novel offer. For 1000 rubles, he could buy all the land he was able to walk around in a day. The only catch in the deal was that he had to be back at his starting point by sundown.

Early the next morning, he started out walking at a quick pace. By midday though tired, he kept going, covering more and more ground. Well into the afternoon, he realized that his greed had taken him far from the starting point. He quickened his pace, and with the sun sinking low in the sky, he began to run, knowing that if he did not make it back by sundown, the opportunity to become an even bigger landholder would be lost.

At sunset, he was within sight of the finish line. Gasping for breath, his heart pounding, he called upon every bit of strength left in his body, and staggered across the line just before the sun disappeared. He immediately collapsed, blood streaming from his mouth. In a few minutes he was dead.

His servants dug his grave. It was not much over 6 feet long and 3 feet wide. The title of Tolstoy's story was: *"How Much Land Does a Man Need?"*[4]

Micah might ask the shop owners and the investment brokers the same question. Their patience for a country preacher questioning their methods and condemning their esurient, insatiable lust for riches, must have been long gone. They may have disdained him, they must have disregarded him, and they surely dismissed him. But they would not so easily cast aside the words of Jehovah God.

"Her wound is incurable".

CHAPTER THREE
IT'S BETTER HIGHER UP!

THE ONLINE ENCYCLOPEDIA, Wikipedia, has an entry entitled the *"List of federal political scandals in the United States".*[5] The list, which seems to be a technological mile long, gives the impression it would be easier and faster to simply record the politicians that were clean and above reproach.

To make matters worse, the editors of Wikipedia added this statement:

"This is an incomplete list, which may never be able to satisfy particular standards for completeness. You can help by expanding it with reliably sourced entries."

One gets the idea that members of the Executive, Legislative, and Judicial branches in Washington D.C. are more than qualified and able to expand that list. Our help, most likely, is not necessary.

Political scandals that have rocked America range from the bizarre to the dangerous. South Carolina governor, Mark Sanford, disappeared for 6 days, finally admitting he had gone to Buenos Aires for an adulterous affair. Louisiana Congressman William Jefferson was convicted on 11 counts of bribery, racketeering, and money laundering. He was found to have a "freezer full of alleged bribe money stuffed in veggie burger boxes".[6] Representative Andrew Weiner of New York took the high tech route, admitting to multiple "inappropriate electronic relationships"[7]. We are daily reminded that ignominy is not reserved to a single political party, nor is it limited to Washington D.C. From small town America to our nation's capital to distant shores, such news hardly seems to surprise us.

Micah lived in a similar day. He understood God expected leadership which would provide its people a standard of fairness and integrity. When they failed, God stood in the courtroom of the skies, and leveled this indictment:

"For the transgression of Jacob is all this, and for the sins of the house of Israel. What is the transgression of Jacob? is it not Samaria? and what are the high places of Judah? are they not Jerusalem" (Micah 1:5)?

The powerful judgments of God described in Micah 1:3-4 would cascade upon the land because of their sins. That retribution would begin at Samaria, the capital of the northern kingdom, and Jerusalem, the southern capital.

The lands were descending into the abyss of sin, and God was holding them accountable. There would be no slick lawyer parsing words now. There would be no campaign ads full of Hollywood glitz and glamour, glossing over sins. Standing at the bar, the all-knowing

Creator of the Universe goes right at the leadership in their entrenched houses of politic. They may escape from the law, they may escape from the people, but they could not escape God.

God promised to turn Samaria into a "heap" (Micah 1:6) - a pile of ruins. Over time, the "heap" would become a reminder to future generations of past glory. To this day, Samaria is still a pile of rubble, telling historians a story of ancient days.

He promised to level the bustling city so that a man could plant a "vineyard" (Micah 1:7). He would push the stones of the buildings "into the valley", and reveal the "foundations". All of their images would be beat "to pieces", the harlots desecrating the house of worship would be "burned with fire", and their idols would be "made desolate". As part of their false religion, they would gift the temple prostitutes in their 'worship'. God told them that money would be confiscated by the enemy, who in turn would use it to pay their own religious harlots.

The rulers had created a mess, and now they would have to 'pay the piper'.

The book of Micah is composed of three messages the man of God preached. The second oracle begins in chapter 3, and Micah wastes no time in making the point. There is no fancy introduction, no funny story, nor does he warm up the crowd. He loads up, finds the target, and fires away.

"Hear, I pray you, O heads of Jacob, and ye princes of the house of Israel" (Micah 3:1). The leaders, judges, and the rulers (the princes) have been ushered into the setting to hear God's accusations.

He starts with a penetrating question. "Is it not for you to know judgment?" Of all people, as leaders they were expected to know the commands and laws of the Bible. God expected them to act fairly, to protect the poor that could not defend themselves, and to execute justice on the wicked that had defrauded them.

The case against them could not have been stronger. Though they knew right, they refused to practice it, and became people that "hate the good, and love the evil". That love was an illicit love, a lusting for evil things that twisted their thinking to the point where they would "call evil good, and good evil" (Isaiah 5:20). With no moral compass, soon they were acting savagely against the very people they were to defend. "Who also eat the flesh of my people, and flay their skin from off them; and they break their bones, and chop them in pieces, as for the pot, and as flesh within the caldron" (Micah 3:3).

The picture was gruesome because the sin was gruesome. The leadership had become spiritual cannibals, preying upon those least able to defend themselves. Some 750 years later, Jesus would call similar people "ravening wolves" in "sheep's clothing" (Matthew 7:15). The Apostle Paul would describe "grievous wolves" seeking to destroy the local church (Acts 20:29).

There was more. Micah exposed them as leaders who "abhor judgment, and pervert all equity" (Micah 3:9). Not surprisingly, at the root of all their evil, was the lust for money, evidenced by their judging "for reward" (Micah 3:11). The votes of the politicians were for sale. The decisions handed down in the courtrooms coincided with the bribes under the table. They were destroying the poor, while building their empires on "blood" money (Micah 3:10).

But God had a judgment for those judges! As their ears were deaf to the humble man pleading for justice in their courtroom, so God would be deaf to their cries for help in His courtroom. "Then shall they cry unto the LORD, but he will not hear them: he will even hide his face from them at that time, as they have behaved themselves ill in their doings" (Micah 3:4). They would reap what they had sown! As their needy victims left the courtrooms destitute, they would experience the horrors they had created. One day, God would see that their "mischief" would return on their own heads (Psalm 7:16). "Whoso stoppeth his ears at the cry of the poor, he also shall cry himself, but shall not be heard" (Proverbs 21:13).

Our day is a desperate day. There is an increasing hopelessness dominating America, as common citizens realize their leaders have no answers. The cancer of cynicism festers throughout the land when corrupt leaders abuse the people they claim to represent. They are recklessly racking up charges on a credit card they seem to think doesn't have a limit. The school systems they have created are dens of danger, physical and emotional halls of ruin for our children. Arrogant judges are making victims out of criminals, and criminals out of victims. Amoral politicians are bent on destroying the family, and calling sodomites married couples.

It has affected God's people. Some are angry, some are frightened, some are complacent, but it has affected us. A

Christian who spends more time with Bill O'Reilly and Rush Limbaugh than with the Lord will end up in a condition of hopelessness. If we convince ourselves the answer is the next election, then we deceive ourselves. The answer is still "repentance toward God, and faith toward our Lord Jesus Christ" (Acts 20:21).

The noted evangelist of a century ago, D.L. Moody, loved to tell the story of an elderly, bed-ridden saint. A Christian lady often visited her and found her quite cheerful. This visitor had a lady friend of wealth who claimed to be a Christian, yet constantly looked on the dark side of things, and was always cast down. She thought it would do this lady good to see the sickly saint, so she brought her to the house.

As the woman lived in an apartment five stories up, there were stairs to climb. At the first story, the woman lifted the bottom of her dress and said, "How dark and filthy it is!"

"It's better higher up," said her friend.

It was no better on the second story. When the lady complained again, her friend replied, "It's better higher up."

Every step seemed to embitter the woman all the more, yet despite the incessant grumbling, her friend kept saying, "It's better higher up."

When they finally reached the fifth story and entered the apartment, they found a clean carpet on the floor, flowering plants in the window, and little birds singing on the balcony. There they found a bed-ridden saint beaming with joy.

The lady said to her, "It must be very hard for you to lie here."

She smiled, then said, "It's better higher up."[8]

It is heartbreaking to watch our nation crumble spiritually. Leaders that claim the name of God while running for election, desecrate that same name with their lifestyles. Justice and judgments are trampled in the street. Despair and desperation are the order of the day. It is almost as if we can hear the voice of Almighty God cry over our land:

"Her wound is incurable".

Yet about that time, Heaven adds another comment:

"It's better higher up!"

CHAPTER FOUR

MAKING THE PEOPLE ERR

IT IS TEMPTING TO LISTEN to Micah blast the greed of the business community and the political community, and respond with a hearty "Amen!" So long as the sinners live on Wall Street, and the corner of Northeast Street and First Street in Washington D.C., (the home of the US Capitol), they are very popular targets.

But there existed another reason the problems were *"incurable"* in the days of Micah, and at the end of the day, it was the most significant reason. When the nation was failing and sin was out of control, when avarice, immorality, and jobbery were rampant, God has always had a stopgap measure. It is the last line of defense, and if it fails, the last hope fizzles with it.

God's preachers have to make the difference.

It happened before. We can open our Bibles and see numerous occasions where the people of God teetered on the edge, only to find a man of God crying out. When the wrath of God was ready to fall upon Israel, Moses "stood in the gate of the camp" (Exodus 32:26). As the people of

God carelessly made a religious vow they might not keep, Joshua told them to choose "this day" whom they would serve (Joshua 24:15). When wicked King Ahab was leading the nation down the highway of hedonism, the mighty prophet Elijah gathered the people "unto mount Carmel" (1 Kings 18:19). Well did Ezekiel thunder heaven's message, "I sought for a man among them, that should make up the hedge, and stand in the gap before me for the land, that I should not destroy it" (Ezekiel 22:30).

When the wheels are coming off, it is not time for new programs, new philosophies, or new prescriptions. Instead of a new idea, the need is an old book. Desperate times call for a righteous man of God standing for His Savior, standing against Satan, standing against sin, and proclaiming "thus saith the Lord".

The reverends in Micah's day did not quite see it like that.

Those ministers were bought and paid for by the godless leadership. When they needed a minister to pray at the inauguration or bless their dirty business, they were readily available. They would not preach against the wicked king, the perverse judges, or the nefarious executives, but it would be a mistake to assume they never preached. There was one target that would raise their blood pressure and get them waxing eloquent. It would be a mistake to say they were for everything and against nothing.

They were against Micah.

"Prophesy ye not, say they to them that prophesy: they shall not prophesy to them" (Micah 2:6). Micah was saying, "They preach at me and say, 'Don't preach at us!'" The only thing they were willing to condemn was a God-called preacher that condemned sin!

Micah has joined some very select company. Notice the word "ye". They were not simply silencing Micah, they were after Isaiah, Hosea, and Urijah (Jeremiah 26:20). Three decades earlier, the 'Ministerial Association of Samaria' told Amos, "Prophesy not against Israel, and drop not thy word against the house of Isaac" (Amos 7:16). Seven centuries later, a choice saint named Stephen would preach so powerfully, they "stopped their ears" (Acts 7:57).

But Micah would not be deterred. He exposed the false ministers who refused to preach a message that would bring "shame" to the wicked (Micah 2:6). They were so refined and dignified, they would never embarrass the thieves that were ransacking the land. They sounded so sanctimonious as they asked, "Is the spirit of the LORD straitened (impatient)" (Micah 2:7)? They were telling people that God would never judge them as Micah said. You can almost hear them break out into song, "He was there all the time; waiting patiently in line."

Their message of false hope soothed the evil man and his conscience, but it did not pacify Almighty God. When a minister preaches a soft message, refusing to condemn sin, he is not attacking a preacher like Micah as much as he is attacking God. Micah called them out on it. They were misquoting and misusing the Bible, so Micah demonstrated how to be accurate with the Word of God. "Do not my words do good to him that walketh uprightly?" That is an accurate reference to verses like Psalm 15:2, Psalm 84:11, and Proverbs 2:7.

They were afraid to denounce sin, but Micah was not. While most people thought their greatest enemy was the Assyrian army, Micah preached of an enemy within their gates. That enemy would "pull off the robe with the garment" (Micah 2:8). The robe referred to an outer garment of dignity worn by a Hebrew man. As Joseph's brothers stripped away his coat and his dignity, these covetous wretches were willing to destroy a man's dignity to make a dollar.

As a conquering soldier returning from the battle thinks himself safe at home, the people thought they were safe in their city walls. Not so. The hoarders on the inside were biding their time to take everything. Imagine an American soldier returning from war discovering the creditors had taken all he had.

These business people went so far as to cheat women (likely widows - perhaps women whose husbands had been sold into slavery) out of their "pleasant houses" (Micah 2:9). Like the Pharisees, they "devour widows' houses" (Mark 12:40). Children no longer had an inheritance because of the crooks.

Micah put the blame right where it belonged. Yes, there were guilty political leaders and guilty businessmen, but in the end, it was all about the guilty ministers. They practiced the worst form of deceit - deceit in the name of God. "If a man walking in the spirit and falsehood do lie" (Micah 2:11) describes a careless attitude toward their calling. They appeared to be so spiritual in their walk and talk, but they were liars. The average church member would be highly offended at the suggestion that ministers lie, but it is so. "The prophets prophesy lies in my name: I sent them not, neither have I commanded them, neither spake unto them: they prophesy unto you a false vision and divination, and a thing of nought, and the deceit of their heart" (Jeremiah 14:14).

Micah is not done. With a stroke of words, he not only castigates the clerics of his day, but the vast majority of our day. The man who promises to "prophesy unto thee of wine and of strong drink; he shall even be the prophet of this people." Instead of a God-called prophet pleading with a wicked people to repent, they wanted a party preacher. "You can have your booze. You can have your good times." In the modern vernacular, it would sound like this: "You can have your best life now!"

Instead of proclaiming "come out from among them, and be ye separate" (2 Corinthians 6:17), the shepherds surveyed their sheep, and then responded by giving them what they desired. They wanted a religious experience that would soothe their conscience, but not a message that would change their lives. They responded to such drivel by installing the popular man who preached a popular sermon as a "prophet of this people." They no longer needed God to call and ordain His prophets, they took the liberty of choosing their own.

God is not done. He accused them of making the "people err" (Micah 3:5); they were leading them astray. It is bad enough when "all we like sheep have gone astray; we have turned every one to his own way" (Isaiah 53:6). If we follow our own thinking and attitudes, we will do a great job of going off course from God and His word. These people had the added 'benefit' of their ministers leading them down the broad road to destruction.

It was customary in Old Testament times to give a gift to the man of God when one was consulting him. Soon that was abused, so that the wealthy man with a better gift would get a better blessing than a poor man with a lesser gift. If someone would give their reverend a good "bite" to eat, he would respond with a wonderful blessing of "Peace". If someone didn't fatten the love offering with a good meal, instead of a blessing there would be a curse of "war" (Micah 3:5.) A commentator put it perfectly. "What came out of the mouth of those prophets depended on what was put into it. Money spoke louder than God."[9]

God would not be compromised. He was not interested in meeting them on their terms. One of the most dangerous pronouncements against them sounded like this, "Therefore night shall be unto you, that ye shall not have a vision; and it shall be dark unto you, that ye shall not divine; and the sun shall go down over the prophets, and the day shall be dark over them" (Micah 3:6). Evidently, there was a day when these prophets had received messages as did Isaiah and Micah, but those days were long gone. Instead of the light of the Word of God showing the path to take (Psalm 119:105), a spiritual darkness descended upon them. The sun had set across the land, and there was no message from God to preach.

A land devoid of the Bible is a land of darkness. It is no coincidence that the darkest places on earth are also places without the liberty the Word of God brings. When the Bible is oppressed the nation is oppressed. When the Bible is in shackles the people are in shackles. When the Bible is mocked the lives of the citizenry are a mockery.

The day was promised when the enemy would invade the land. There would come a time when the ministers would seek the Lord, when the people would need Him, yet they would discover that He is not a god on the end of a marionette string. When they needed Him most, they would realize "there is no answer of God" (Micah 3:7).

No answer! One day the false minister, who fattens his wallet by cheapening the Bible, will look to Heaven. One day the diabolical cleric, who deceives his parishioners with a false gospel, will seek the truth. One day the dishonest seminary professor, who ridicules the Bible and its miracles, will seek such a miracle from Heaven.

On that day there will be no answer! Times of judgment fill the Bible when the Lord ignores the pleas of a shocked society. They discover only too late that God is not there all the time. Mercy is great, but it is not endlessly available.

"He, that being often reproved hardeneth his neck, shall suddenly be destroyed, and that without remedy" (Proverbs 29:1).

No remedy. No answer. No cure.

A hunter raised his rifle and took careful aim at a large bear. When he was about to pull the trigger, the bear spoke in a soft, soothing voice, "Isn't it better to talk than to shoot? What do you want? Let's negotiate the matter." Lowering his rifle, the hunter replied, "I want a fur coat."

"Good," said the bear, "we can find a solution. I only want a full stomach, so let us negotiate a compromise."

They sat down to discuss the problem, and after a time the bear walked away alone. The negotiations had been successful. The bear had a full stomach, and the hunter had his fur coat.[10]

Many a preacher has compromised with the bear. He changes his message, weakens his convictions, and looks the other way. Humanly speaking, the negotiations with the world have been very successful. But the bear walks away as the winner.

By then, *"her wound is incurable"*.

CHAPTER FIVE

WHAT DOES THE LORD REQUIRE?

IN 1978, MARSHALL CUMMINGS of Tulsa, Oklahoma, was accused of purse snatching. He chose to be his own lawyer. While cross-examining the victim, he asked, "Did you get a good look at my face when I took your purse?"[11] A state jury convicted Cummings of attempted robbery by force and gave him a ten year prison sentence, proving once again, that a "man who is his own lawyer has a fool for a client."[12]

An eminent New York lawyer, Francis Wellmann, wrote a treatise on the *"Art of Cross-examination"*. He detailed the qualities that make a successful interrogator:

"It requires the greatest ingenuity; a habit of logical thought; clearness of perception in general; infinite patience and self-control; power to read men's minds intuitively, to judge their characters by their faces, to appreciate their motives; ability to act with force and precision; a masterful knowledge of the subject matter itself; and extreme caution; and, above all, the instinct to discover the weak point in the witness under examination."[13]

The good counselor would have fascinated by Micah 6.

The trial of Israel and Judah moves along, and it is time for Almighty God to cross-examine the witness. The command of God is, "Arise, contend" (Micah 6:1). Contend is a legal word befitting the trial for the ages. The people of God are to stand up and answer the affidavit that is the book of Micah.

Unusual witnesses are called to the trial. The "mountains" and the "strong foundations of the earth" (Micah 6:2) will attest to the truth. It would be easy to dismiss this statement as exaggeration, but that would be a grave error. Jesus said that stones have the ability to "cry out" (Luke 19:40), and Joshua once set a great stone before the people, telling them it had heard their promises to God. Should they deny God, that stone would "witness" against them (Joshua 24:27).

Those very stones and hills listened as their forefathers promised to honor and follow the commands of God. Now, God was ready to call them to the witness stand to prove His case. It is unnerving in the least to consider such a thing. Should God call His creation to testify against us, not a one would be able to stand.

While they anxiously twist and turn, God has some questions to ask. "What have I done unto thee? and wherein have I wearied thee" (Micah 6:3)? He tells them to "testify" to His actions. In case they were tongue-tied, He is ready to help. He "brought (them) up out of the land of Egypt, and redeemed (them) out of the house of servants;

and I sent before (them) Moses, Aaron, and Miriam" (Micah 6:4). He asks them if He has "wearied" them (made their life heavy and miserable). In fact, He had made them light and free.

When Pharaoh enslaved them, He redeemed them. When Balaam tried to curse them, God chose to bless them. On both sides of the Jordan, Shittim and Gilgal, God pampered, protected, and provided for them. He never let them down. His "righteousness" was always perfect and it always met the need. So the time has come to "testify" and explain their rebellion against God.

The defendant responds. "Wherewith shall I come before the LORD" (Micah 6:6)? What a great question! How can I approach God? How can I please God? Humans are rarely concerned with pleasing God unless they are in desperate need of God. When life is good, when there is money in the bank, when the freezer is full, we normally forget God. It is when the wheels are coming off that we are finally ready to do things His way.

There is a recess to the trial. For a moment, the ever merciful God of the Bible halts the proceedings. The Great Teacher is always ready to reward those who "diligently seek him" (Hebrews 11:6). If they would seek God, if we would seek God, we must first understand what God does not want, then we must recognize what God desires.

Offerings are not the answer. They think if they come with "burnt offerings", or with a year old calf (considered the prime sacrifice and most valuable), that God will be pleased (Micah 6:6). They assume that God can be bought off just as their judges and prophets were bought off. They have convinced themselves that God has His price, but He is not looking for their offering.

Quantity is not the answer. "If God will not accept our offering, perhaps we can impress Him with a larger offering. Let's try 1,000 rams. Let's try 10,000 rivers of oil in our sacrifice." Religion hasn't changed these 26 centuries. It still convinces itself that God will look the other way so long as the ministry is big enough. But God has never been moved by numbers. He is able to "save by many or by few" (1 Samuel 14:6).

Compromise is not the answer. The pagan religions in Micah's day demanded the offering of a son upon the altar. King Ahaz, the father of the present King Hezekiah, chose to convert to the religion of the Assyrian empire, offering his son to the false god Baal. Now the confused citizens of Judah wonder, "Shall I give my firstborn for my transgression, the fruit of my body for the sin of my soul" (Micah 6:7)?

How far were the people of God from the heart of God! When a land is full of compromised, soft preachers, the people have no knowledge of God. The responsibility falls on the shoulders of those ministers that refuse to preach the holiness of God, the fear of God, and the wrath of God. Ultimately, "there is no fear of God before their eyes" (Romans 3:18). They had convinced themselves that God was for sale, and worse, that God was no different than Baal!

We are watching the same tragedy play out in America. Decades of TV evangelism, religious schools full of liberal professors, and mega businesses masquerading as churches, have resulted in a people with no idea who God is or what God wants. Instead, they are convinced that God exists to cater to them.

As a result, they choose a church that plays the music 'I like'. They walk into a religious book store and buy a Bible version that 'I like'. They listen to the minister who will tell them what 'I like'. 'I like' is more important than what 'God wants'. When we arrive at the last act of that play, we will have a generation who thinks the God of the Bible is the same as the Muslim god, the Mormon god, or the Buddhist god.

God did not desire their offerings, their bigger offerings, or their compromise, but there was something He wanted. In fact, it was something He "require(d)" of them (Micah 6:8). How offended the people in Micah's day must have been when they were told that God had expectations from them. How offended most would be today.

Micah 6:8 appears as the motto on the wall of the reading room in the Congressional Library. Evidently, our leadership in Congress doesn't do much reading. The rabbis who commented on this verse in the early centuries of the Christian era called it a one-line summary of the whole Law.[14] It is a verse beautiful in its simplicity.

"He hath shewed thee, O man, what is good; and what doth the LORD require of thee, but to do justly, and to love mercy, and to walk humbly with thy God?"

God wants people who "do justly". He does not want them to promise justice, to talk about justice, or to analyze justice. He wants them to do it.

He wants them to "love mercy". He does not want them to demand mercy of others, He wants His people to love and demonstrate it personally.

He wants them to "walk humbly". If they would understand the privilege of being a child of God and swallow their pride, they could have the joy of walking "with" God. What a generous invitation!

The recess is over and the trial continues. Called to stand at the bar are the inhabitants of the capital city, Jerusalem. God's voice is crying out to the city, and there is someone God is looking for. He seeks for a man of "wisdom", who perceives the power and glory of His "name". Somewhere in the city of 24,000 people there must be a man that will respond to the "rod" of chastisement, and to the God who is brandishing that rod (Micah 6:9).

The rod of chastisement is never a pretty thing. We are reminded "whom the Lord loveth he chasteneth, and scourgeth every son whom he receiveth. If ye endure chastening, God dealeth with you as with sons; for what son is he whom the father chasteneth not" (Hebrews 12:6-7)? Because He loves He disciplines.

Jerusalem would learn what we as a people of God learn. There is only so far we will stray from Him before He will lovingly bring us back. The Spirit of God convicts us internally. Our pastor preaches that perfect message just for us. But if we do not respond, there is the rod of God, a rod that can be harsh.

God promised to make them "sick". The Assyrian army would one day surround, and then starve the city. God would see that they would be "desolate", a sad promise that came to pass when Babylon ultimately destroyed the city (Micah 6:13). In that day, there would be mass starvation, and the little amounts of food they would eat would cause dysentery. There would be painful miscarriages, and the little ones that managed to survive childbirth would die by the sword (Micah 6:14).

They would work hard in sowing their seed, but they would not reap the harvest. They would crush the olives to make the oil, yet never use that oil. They would gather their grapes, but the wine from the presses would be drunk by someone else (Micah 6:15). All of their work and plans would come to nought.

It is always the way with sin. There has to be the wages. It is easy to join Jerusalem of old, and convince ourselves that our troubles are a trial to test us, or perhaps the devil is after us. It is unusual to see a Christian humble himself under the correction of God, and repent before the Lord. When God warns a church that some of its members are weak and sickly, and others have died prematurely as a result of sin, we find a way to ignore Him. How much wiser it would be to "judge ourselves" (1 Corinthians 11:31-32) before He judges us.

Judah had yet another choice to make. Instead of seeking God as David did, or loving God as Solomon did, they determined to follow the wicked examples of their brothers to the north. King Omri and and his son Ahab became their heroes. Omri loved vanities, and his people followed his lust for empty things. Ahab loved himself, and with the help of his wife Jezebel, installed the religion of Baalism in the land. When the folks down south heard of their exploits, they assumed their boring lives of worshipping Jehovah were missing something. Instead of going to the Bible, they went to these wicked kings for their "counsels" (Micah 6:16).

How blind they were! They could not add it up and see that the sin of their brothers up north had brought the wrath of God upon them. By following Omri and Ahab, they would become a "desolation" as well, and soon they would be hissed at (derided), and bear the reproach.

Are we blind also? Can't a Christian teenager understand that following the ungodly rebel at school will only produce a life of shame and disgrace? Can't a Christian lady see that following the styles and attitudes of the Hollywood elitists will only beget a life as miserable as those on display there? Can't a Christian father see that living for vanities and empty pleasures only engenders a lust for more barren waste land?

When will we decide to get off the treadmill? When do we understand that enough is enough? What level of judgment do we face from God before we comprehend this world is not our home?

J.D. Weido is a wonderful pastor, presently serving in El Dorado, Arkansas. I have been privileged to preach with him on a number of occasions, and I am always encouraged by his gracious heart for God and love for the Savior.

Pastor Weido is a man with a tender heart. I am quite certain that he cannot give the announcements without shedding a tear. When I am preaching with him, I am often reminded of the condition of my own cold heart.

On one occasion, I had finished the message, the invitation had concluded, and Brother Weido was closing the service. I will never forget him standing before the church with monster tears rolling down his cheeks, begging the people to repent of their sins, and return to the Lord. Then, in 'Arkansas speak', he told them this, "If we keep on doin' the things we have been doin', then we are going to keep on gettin' the things we've been gettin'".

Exactly right.

If we like what we have been getting in our lives, our marriages, our families, and our churches, then let's keep doing what we have been doing. But if we don't like what we have been getting, then it is time to respond to the pleading of God, before we face the anger of God. When the judgment of God finally comes, it may be we realize a horror Jerusalem heard centuries ago.

We may just discover, *"her wound is incurable"*.

The Prescription

I charge thee therefore before God, and the Lord Jesus Christ, who shall judge the quick and the dead at his appearing and his kingdom; Preach the word; be instant in season, out of season; reprove, rebuke, exhort with all longsuffering and doctrine.

(2 Timothy 4:1-2)

CHAPTER SIX

"BUT AFTER THAT"

DURING THE REIGN OF QUEEN VICTORIA, the wife of a common laborer lost her baby. Having experienced deep sorrow herself, she called on the bereaved woman to comfort her. After she left, the neighbors asked what the queen had said.

"Nothing," replied the grieving mother. "She simply put her hands on mine, and we silently wept together."[15]

The prophet Micah would understand. Like a widow that lost her loved one, Micah was about to lose his country. God had placed that final word over his people.

"For her wound is incurable".

In an instant, a load of emotions must have overwhelmed him. Anger, terror, anguish, remorse, and countless other reactions doubtlessly led to the inevitable human questions. "Why?" "How could a God of love do such a thing?" "How long do we have?"

"Incurable" is a crushing word overruling every plan, every hope, every wish. With one word, financial investments don't seem so important. It doesn't matter

who wins the next Super Bowl. The next election loses urgency.

"Incurable" changes priorities. There is a new prism to view the world, a prism with a very different timetable. Surfing the internet isn't quite as important as spending time with a grandchild. Talking matters but twittering doesn't. Making another dollar loses significance, but witnessing to a lost colleague moves to the head of the line.

At last, we find a way to make time to pray. Fleshly sins don't seem quite as attractive now. The 'wish list' has a few changes to it, and limited time means we will finally do what we know truly matters.

The word *"incurable"* drove Micah to his knees. "I will wail and howl, I will go stripped and naked: I will make a wailing like the dragons, and mourning as the owls" (Micah 1:8). The words in the verse are associated with funerals and grieving for the dead. The man of God tossed off his shoes walking barefoot, as David did when he lost his baby. Like Isaiah and Peter, Micah ripped away his outer and inner robe, leaving only the loincloth.

To say Micah cried would miss the point, as his sorrow went much deeper. Like a dragon (a jackal in the jungle), like an owl, Micah spent the entire night moaning and wailing. There was no sleep for him.

While we might wear black, seclude ourselves, and softly cry, Micah and his people were far more public. Such is the condition of a man that has lost what he loves. Such is the condition *"incurable"*.

One of the most convicting, penetrating songs asks the questions:

How long has it been, since you talked to the Lord,
And told Him your heart's hidden secrets?
How long since you prayed,
How long since you stayed,
On your knees 'til the light shone through?
How long has it been since your mind felt at ease,
How long since your heart knew no burden?[16]

Perhaps we might add the question, "How long has it been since our heart was broken for the sins of the land?" There are many reactions to sin. Some people laugh demonstrating that "fools make a mock at sin" (Proverbs 14:9). Often, we are angered by the unchecked wickedness that seems so ubiquitous. Worse, we can become calloused to sin, and when it is so pervasive, we simply shrug it off and find a way to ignore it.

Sin needs to break our hearts.

When the heart of the Savior saw Jerusalem, it broke. He cried, "O Jerusalem, Jerusalem, thou that killest the prophets, and stonest them which are sent unto thee, how often would I have gathered thy children together, even as a hen gathereth her chickens under her wings, and ye would not" (Matthew 23:37)! "When he saw the multitudes, he was moved with compassion on them, because they fainted, and were scattered abroad, as sheep having no shepherd" (Matthew 9:36).

His compassionate heart felt the lonely exile of the leper and it moved Him. When the sick and the blind and the deaf and the lame told Him their stories, it affected Him. When He saw lost people aimlessly wander through the wilderness of life without a pastor to shepherd them, he cared. When the masses were hungry, it moved Him to the point of feeding them. When He saw the woman following the casket carrying the remains of her son, He not only wiped her tears away, He took away the sting of death.

Jesus knew "what was in man" (John 2:25) and it moved him. When He was "moved", it meant that he felt a deep pity and concern in the depths of His soul. He didn't simply feel sorry for them and their disconsolate condition, He did something about it. He was willing to bare their blindness, their lameness, their deafness, and their leprosy. Yet, the greatest act of mercy and love this world has ever witnessed transpired at Calvary. There Jesus did something far greater than bare our burden, our sicknesses, or our needs. He bore our sins.

"Who his own self bare our sins in his own body on the tree, that we, being dead to sins, should live unto righteousness: by whose stripes ye were healed" (1 Peter 2:24).

The song so beautifully describes His love:

> *And can it be that I should gain*
> *An interest in the Savior's blood?*
> *Died He for me, who caused His pain?*
> *For me, who Him to death pursued?*
> *No condemnation now I dread;*
> *I am my Lord's and He is mine:*
> *Alive in Him, my living Head,*
> *And clothed in righteousness divine.*

Amazing love! How can it be
That thou, my God, shouldst die for me?[17]

One day, Jesus saw us as sinners bound for Hell. We chose to reject Him and His Word. "For we ourselves also were sometimes foolish, disobedient, deceived, serving divers lusts and pleasures, living in malice and envy, hateful, and hating one another" (Titus 3:3).

What a precise, pessimistic, petrifying, declaration. We may fool a parent, a spouse, a pastor, but God knows our desperately wicked condition. Each word in that verse drives the nail into our spiritual coffins all the deeper, ringing the word "guilty" all the louder. Not just sinful. Not just wicked. Not just lost.

"Incurable".

Yet, Titus 3:4 begins with three extraordinary words. "But after that." After the description of our wasted, selfish condition, after the portrayal of our stubborn rebellion, the Savior was "moved". After all of that, "the kindness and love of God our Saviour toward man appeared." After all of that, He went to Calvary to die for our sin. After all of that, He tells us to toss off the notion that we can work our way to Heaven. After all of that, He wants to extend "mercy" (Titus 3:5).

Amazing love! How can it be that Thou, my God, shouldst die for me?

If our *"incurable"* condition drove Jesus to the Cross, perhaps the *"incurable"* condition of our land should drive us to our knees.

CHAPTER SEVEN

EVERY MONDAY MORNING!

IN 1939, RONALD REAGAN starred in a film called "Code of the Secret Service", playing the role of a tough agent named Brass Brancroft. It wasn't his finest moment. The film's producer, Bryan Foy, wanted to shelve the film before it was released. One of the kinder reviews described it as "not very interesting", and Ronald Reagan called it the "worse picture I ever made."[18]

To say the movie was universally condemned would not be accurate. Jerry Parr was a ten year old boy living in Miami who loved the film. He made his father take him to see it repeatedly, and was so impressed, that he determined one day he would be a secret service agent.

Forty-two years later, on March 30, 1982, Secret Service agent Jerry Parr was on detail guarding President Reagan. As assassin John Hinckley opened fire, Parr braved the hailstorm of bullets, tackled the president, and shoved him into the limousine. Speeding toward the White House, it was Parr who saw Mr. Reagan spitting up blood, and he made the instant decision to change course for the hospital, a decision that saved the life of the Ronald Reagan.[19]

Little did Ronald Reagan realize that his worst hour would one day save his life.

Bible preachers have been there. Many a man of God has gone home from a Sunday service wondering if anyone was impacted. He will spend hours pouring over the Word of God, praying for wisdom and direction, and preach from his very soul. Church members never realize the physical, emotional, and spiritual exhaustion their pastors endure to declare God's Word. There is an unseen spiritual battle anytime the Bible is preached, and it is God's man that has the bullseye right on his back.

It wearies a man to preach his heart and see no tangible results. I once made the mistake of asking a pastor if he ever thought about quitting. He gave me a long, incredulous look, shook his head, and said, "Only every Monday morning."

Amos knew the feeling. He was minding his own business in the hills of Tekoa, shepherding his flock, and tending his sycamore trees. Then the call of God came upon him. "Go, prophesy unto my people Israel" (Amos 7:15).

He must have been stunned! After all, his own testimony would say, "I was no prophet, neither was I a prophet's son; but I was an herdman, and a gatherer of sycamore fruit" (Amos 7:14). Who would listen to such a man?

When we have surrendered our lives to God, He will impress on our hearts the "what" of His will. It may be our own Bible study, the message of a pastor, a season in prayer, or more likely, a combination that God uses. After the "what" comes the "where" and the "when". It was the "where" that must have floored Amos. God wanted him to leave the little village of Tekoa, travel 19 miles due north to the capital of their compromised religion, Bethel, and preach some of the most provoking and powerful messages in the Old Testament.

The country preacher may have wondered aloud at such a call! Yet, a man of God is simply a chosen vessel. It is a privilege to be "put in trust with the gospel" (1 Thessalonians 2:4), so he soldiers on. When we surrender to God, He gets to tell us "what" and "where" and "when".

Amos comes to the land of Israel to the north. The first words out of his mouth set the stage, "The LORD will roar from Zion" (Amos 1:2). For the rest of the book of Amos, he roars the message of God.

He opens the book by naming their sins. There is no soft peddling here. They had cheapened life, they had abused the poor, and they loved their booze. In chapter three, they were so hardened, they couldn't see the difference between right and wrong. Their opulence and greed stifled any interest in God. Covetousness ruled the day.

Amos is just warming up. In chapter four he condemns their avarice and exposes their hypocritical religion. He uncovers their spiritual dullness demonstrating their unwillingness to respond to the judgment of God. Because they would not respond to preaching and chastisement, he tells them the time has come to "prepare to meet thy God, O Israel" (Amos 4:12).

Chapter five describes their love of false religion, describing a people that would bow their knee to false idols and gods. In chapter six, he calls out their indifference and complacency. In case they missed it the first time, the Billy Sunday of that day put the liquor crowd in their place yet again.

God was just beginning. In Amos 7:1, the 'word' of the Lord became the 'vision' of the Lord. Amos did not simply hear the message God wanted him to preach, he saw the message. Five visions describe the powerful wrath of God ready to fall upon a people who had rejected His mercy. When Amos told them God had a standard and they had failed to live up to God's standard, he struck a nerve, and the fat hit the fire.

"Then Amaziah the priest of Bethel sent to Jeroboam king of Israel, saying, Amos hath conspired against thee in the midst of the house of Israel: the land is not able to bear all his words. For thus Amos saith, Jeroboam shall die by the sword, and Israel shall surely be led away captive out of their own land" (Amos 7:10-11).

The good doctor decided enough was enough. He sent a message to the king, informing his highness that the ministerial association had passed a resolution condemning the negative message of the hillbilly minister from Tekoa. Then, the head priest, Amaziah, turned his vitriol on Amos.

"Also Amaziah said unto Amos, O thou seer, go, flee thee away into the land of Judah, and there eat bread, and prophesy there: But prophesy not again any more at Bethel: for it is the king's chapel, and it is the king's court" (Amos 7:12-13).

Amaziah would have been welcome at the denominational headquarters in our land! He would have been well received by spiritually dead Seminary professors, with their delicate messages and cushy beliefs. He would have no problem filling a schedule in the liberal establishments mocking a hick preacher's message and style. The elitists reviled Amos, just as the false teachers of our day ridicule a man who actually preaches the Bible as it is to men as they are.

Amos would not be deterred. When told that his preaching would no longer be tolerated, the man of God gave a parting message. "Now therefore hear thou the word of the LORD: Thou sayest, Prophesy not against Israel, and drop not thy word against the house of Isaac. Therefore thus saith the LORD; Thy wife shall be an harlot in the city, and thy sons and thy daughters shall fall by the sword, and thy land shall be divided by line; and thou shalt die in a polluted land: and Israel shall surely go into captivity forth of his land" (Amos 7:16-17).

Imagine Amos returning to Tekoa. Ringing in his ears were the taunts and threats of those who hated him and his message. Some preachers are better than others at pretending not to care, but every man of God is affected by hostility and rejection. His confidence is shattered, and it takes a load of grace and courage to step in the pulpit again.

In the friendly confines of Tekoa, Amos is going to give the missions report. The trip to Bethel was a failure. No one listened and no one responded. He poured out his soul, he put his life, his reputation, his finances, his all on the line, and he came back empty. I can see him preaching yet again, wondering if the crowd at Tekoa will respond.

But there was a young man, perhaps a teenager. He lived 17 ½ miles away in another little place called Moresh. If mom and dad cared enough to give him a name reminding him that no one else was like Jehovah God, it is very likely they may have taken their boy on a trip to Tekoa to hear the man of God. Preachers like Micah do not learn to preach from a book. They do not learn to preach from a professor. They learn to preach from someone like Amos.

Imagine a discouraged Amos wondering if it is worth it. "Why should I keep preaching? Why don't I just quit?" Perhaps he found himself wondering if Doctor Amaziah was right. "Maybe I should just go and flee away. I get more respect from my flock of sheep than I do from flocks of sinners."

Yet, there are many reasons for a man to keep on preaching, one of which is that young teenager who may be out there listening. A young Elisha learned from Elijah. Obadiah, Joel, and perhaps even Jonah may have listened to Elisha preach. A young Hosea and an even younger Isaiah may have joined Micah listening to Amos. It is very possible that Jeremiah, Habbakuk, Ezekiel, and perhaps a little guy named Daniel sat at the feet of one of the greatest revival preachers in the Bible, Zephaniah.

That is the mystery of preaching. We never know. Even when we think we know, we don't know. After 30 years of evangelism, I often meet men who were called to preach in a service years ago. I don't remember the meeting. I don't remember the topic, but there is a great spiritual pleasure when someone comes up and says, "One day I heard the message God had you preach, and I responded to do the will of God."

"So shall my word be that goeth forth out of my mouth: it shall not return unto me void, but it shall accomplish that which I please, and it shall prosper in the thing whereto I sent it" (Isaiah 55:11).

In the darkest days, when all hope seems to be gone, it is impossible to know what God is doing. Even when it appears that Heaven is silent, and nothing is happening, He is working behind the scenes. He may simply be repositioning a pawn on the board, but the end result is a checkmate of Satan's devices. He knows what He is doing.

It is the reason we cannot get discouraged. It is the reason we cannot surrender. Even when the situation is *"incurable"*.

CHAPTER EIGHT

A DIFFERENT KIND OF PREACHING

"For her wound is incurable". The message that drove Micah to his knees, is now going to drive Micah to the pulpit.

One of the most common questions young, sincere, Christian men ask is this, "How do I know if God has called me to preach?" The answer is always the same, and it is always frustrating. "If you are called to preach, you will know." The advice through the ages has always been, "If you can do something other than preach, you probably should."

Preaching is not a job. Preaching is not a profession. Preaching is not a hobby. Preaching is a life. The Apostle Paul said it best. "For though I preach the gospel, I have nothing to glory of: for necessity is laid upon me; yea, woe is unto me, if I preach not the gospel" (1 Corinthians 9:16)! We do not preach for our own glory, but for His glory. We preach out of necessity (a compelling force).

That "necessity" describes the prophet's condition in Micah 1:10. Micah stands to his feet, wipes the tears away, grits his teeth, and decides to preach. One can almost feel the volcano of his soul begin to rumble, the passion of his heart stirring. The fire that burned in the heart of Elijah on Mount Carmel begins to rage in his heart. The passion that loosened the tongue of Micaiah in the palace of Ahab is about to set his message free. The fearlessness of John the Baptist in the wilderness is ready to dominate him. "If it is *'incurable'*, and if there truly is no hope, then I have a choice to make."

If Micah was going down, he was going down preaching.

In Micah's day, there were 46 cities and towns surrounding the capital city of Jerusalem. The day would come when the Assyrian king Sennacherib would lead a march of destruction conquering those villages. Micah had his own 'march'.

Micah 1:10-16 details ten locales whose people received a message from the man of God. When he is called upon to give his testimony in Heaven, it would not be at all surprising to discover that he preached in all 46 places. When a man has a burden, when God has told him the wound is *"incurable"*, there is no reason to limit the itinerary.

The theme of his preaching was fascinating, as he constructs and delivers a message exposing their city name. Perhaps he found himself in the city square, by the 'welcome to' sign, or in another place of congregation, and as he thunders his message, he is preaching to their identity. It is their name that makes them distinct, that gives them connection with generations past, and gives them a sense of civic pride. Micah informs them God's judgment will put an end to their comfortable, small town life.   .

Micah travels six miles away to a city called Gath, the closest Philistine city to Judah, and repeats a message their forefathers heard some 250 years earlier. When King Saul and his beloved son Jonathan were killed, a mournful David lamented over them, crying, "Tell it not in Gath, publish it not in the streets of Askelon" (2 Samuel 1:20). In his hour of sorrow, David could not bear the thought of Philistine laughter and rejoicing at the death of Israel's leaders. Now Micah repeats that message. "Declare ye it not at Gath, weep ye not at all" (Micah 1:10). Micah stands in the middle of their city reminding them of the day they laughed at God and His people. Now they were in the crosshairs of the the judgment of God, and, this time there would no laughter. There is nothing at all humorous about the wrath of God.

God's man moves on to an insignificant, anonymous town called the House of Aphrah. The word 'Aphrah' means dust. We might well call it Dust-town, giving us a picture of a western town, with its tumbleweed blowing across the dusty streets. The preacher solemnly announces that when God has passed by, they would be rolling "in the dust". In Bible times, it was considered a sign of mourning to place dust on one's head, so the picture of an entire village wallowing in the dust would describe sorrow of enormous intensity.

Stop number three on the itinerary was a wonderful place called Saphir. The word means beautiful, pleasant, so we might well translate it as Pleasanton, a common name for American towns. Life was about to take a cruel turn for these citizens, as they were soon to "pass away", a phrase meaning to be carried away unwillingly. When the Assyrian king Sennacherib invaded the land, some 200,000 prisoners from places like Saphir were captured. Micah pictured them being led away shamed and naked. Not so pleasant.

Zaanan was a town for shepherds, its name meaning to "go out". Its original name described the flocks that would go in and out of the village. Now, their city name carried a message their lives would depend upon, for when the enemy attacked, they would have to get out and run for their lives.

Bethezel was the "house on the side" or the next door neighbor. The name gives a picture of standing firm and strong, but that would mean nothing when the mighty enemy would "receive of you" (take them away from their safety).

The people of Maroth (Bitter-town) were an anxious people who "waited carefully for good." They were hoping against hope that they would be spared from the enemy invasion, but the Lord knew their location. Bitter-town would know a bitter end.

Lachish (Impregnable-town) was one of the largest cities outside of Jerusalem, located some 6 miles from Moresh. King Rehoboam built the city to be impregnable (the meaning of the name) with a massive wall some 20 feet thick. It stood on the road to Jerusalem to protect the capital city. The people had convinced themselves their military advantages would win the day, but that confidence was only the beginning of her downfall. A city may have a great army and impressive fortifications, but if they tolerate idolatry and sin, they are no match for God. Micah told them to tie their chariots to the swift beasts in order to escape the impending judgment. Instead of harnessing the war horses, they were to use the race horses. They would not be fighting. They would be fleeing.

Micah's next stop was his home village of Moresheth. One of the hardest places to preach is back home, as Jesus words and experience prove; "A prophet is not without honour, but in his own country, and among his own kin, and in his own house" (Mark 6:4). Moresh means a town of inheritance. Micah may have grown up thinking his hometown was a special inheritance, a distinguished gift. When the enemy came, however, Moresh would be a present (a parting gift) to them, and their valuable inheritance would be forever gone to the hands of their feared enemy.

Achzib would translate as "Lie-town" or "Deception-town", and it would serve as a "lie to the kings of Israel". They hoped that the citizens from the houses of Achzib would be there to help battle Assyria, but the houses were empty of soldiers. The city looked promising, but those looks were truly deceiving.

The tenth city was Mareshah. Its name means to be at the head and possess, a play on the word "conqueror". The conquerors would be conquered. The possessors would be possessed. They would have to run and hide in the cave of Adullam as David did when all hope was gone.

What preaching! Courageously, fearlessly, Micah erases their self confidence and security. The judgment of God was closer than they realized, and there was no place to hide from Him.

We might imagine Micah preaching in America. See him standing next to the famous "Hollywood" sign, the pride and joy of Tinseltown - Los Angeles, California. The business of Hollywood has piped its immorality, its profanity, and its rebellion into living rooms around the world. It would certainly be an appropriate place for Micah to start his American tour:

"The name 'Hollywood' means the place of evergreens and berries. When God is finished, there will be nothing but barrenness and emptiness. All of the phony pretense that make up image of this city will be exposed for what it is."

He might make his way to my home town of Phoenix, Arizona. "The word Phoenix means to rise from the ashes. When the wrath of God falls upon this city, it will be burned to ashes again!"

Listen to Micah stand in the godless den called Bourbon Street in New Orleans. "The 'golden' city of New Orleans with its abundance of pleasures and sin have an appointment with God! Let the good times roll? When the judgment of God comes, your Mardi Gras parades will wind their way to Hell!"

Perhaps he would pay a visit to the morally repugnant South Beach of Miami. "Miami? The name means 'sweet water', but when God deals with your wickedness, the sweet waters will turn bitter!"

"Philadelphia! The city of brotherly love will become the city of hatred!"

"Chicago! Your name came from a word meaning 'skunk place'. You won't bear the smell of the judgment of God!"

"Cleveland! The 'land of the cliff' will be falling off the cliff!"

This is not the preaching that is taught in the seminaries and homiletics classes. This is not the preaching pulpit committees are looking for. This is not the preaching of a slick TV minister, whose biggest worry is keeping the coffers full. This is not the preaching of an hireling worried about paying the mortgage. This is not the preaching of an up and coming reverend climbing the denominational ladder.

This is the preaching of man who heard from God that time is running out. This is the preaching that causes a man of God to tell the people to mourn like they had never before: "Make thee bald, and poll thee for thy delicate children; enlarge thy baldness as the eagle." This is the preaching of a man that has watched his brothers up north go "into captivity", and he knows his own people are marching to the same beat.

This is the kind of message a man preaches when the situation is *"incurable"*.

CHAPTER NINE

FULL PREACHERS

IN 2010, I WAS PRIVILEGED to preach in Papua New Guinea with Missionary Gary Keck. One of the opportunities took me to the second largest city of PNG, the city of Lae, where I met a pastor named Jacob Kepas. When I asked him for his testimony, he responded with a compelling story.

Pastor Kepas had a promising career working for an oil company, a claim very few can make in a such a destitute country. When the Lord saved him, he was soon burdened for the friends in his home village, but the religious authorities would have none of it. When he preached at the open air market, they interrupted him, destroying his sound equipment. They promised if he dared return, they would do to him as they had done to the gear.

The following week, Pastor Kepas returned to preach. The religious authorities kept their word, beating him mercilessly, and breaking his nose. They threatened his life if he returned with his Bible.

He would not be deterred. Yet again, that bold man of God declared the marvelous plan of Salvation. As the authorities marched down the street to confront him, a group from the market abruptly surged to his defense. Over time, many in that same crowd responded to the Gospel of Christ, and became the foundation of a new church.

The pulpit is no place for a lightweight. It may be common for an unsaved world to scoff, spurn, or sneer at someone like Micah, but there is nothing tranquil about the labor of a Bible preacher. There is a heavy personal, financial, and physical cost a man of God pays. He does so without reluctance, for there was a day when he joined the Apostle Paul is testifying, "So, as much as in me is, I am ready to preach the gospel to you that are at Rome also" (Romans 1:15). "No one forced me. No one obliged me. Of my own ready mind, I willingly surrendered to do anything, to go anywhere, only that God's will may be done in my life."

When a man like Micah, or Paul, or Jacob Kepas chooses to preach for God, they readily move themselves into the background. He tells them what to do, where to go, and what to say, and, like John the Baptist, they simply become a "voice" (Mark 1:3). Read the prophets of the Bible and you will see very little about their personal lives. They are very careful in their preaching so that the message of God is central, not their thinking. You will never see, "I said so." You will see, "Thus saith the Lord."

It makes Micah 3:8 a very special verse.

"But truly I am full of power by the spirit of the LORD, and of judgment, and of might, to declare unto Jacob his transgression, and to Israel his sin." When a man is Spirit filled, he will be strong enough to stand against pressures to compromise, he will have a thirst for righteousness, he will be brave, and he will preach. He will be a pariah to the world, for he will represent a type of minister they have never seen, a man that makes them uncomfortable.

Churches that once stood strong for the Bible seem to be compromising on all sides, as modern ministers follow the path of least resistance. It seems to the average member that no one is left, and everyone has caved. But that is not so. While the rest of the ministers were following the easy path of concession, Micah chose a different route. So did Amos. So did Michaiah. So did John the Baptist. So did Paul. Not everyone is caving to the world.

Repeatedly, the Bible demands that its preachers take a stand against this world and its thinking. To his disciples, Jesus said, "If ye were of the world, the world would love his own: but because ye are not of the world, but I have chosen you out of the world, therefore the world hateth you" (John 15:19). It was the expectation of Christ that His representatives would shun the approval of the unsaved. Their acknowledgment was not only unwarranted, it was also unwanted. It is impossible to preach a narrow way to Heaven, and a narrow standard for right, and still be popular.

"Woe unto you, when all men shall speak well of you! for so did their fathers to the false prophets" (Luke 6:26).

A strong preacher is a man submitted to the Spirit of God, yearning to be a vessel empty of self and full of Him. By submitting to the Holy Spirit, Micah became the quintessential example of a man of God. His brief testimony in Micah 3:8 describes the transformation in his life:

He was full of power. God gave him the strength to travel the land preaching a message of judgment. When a man is full of the Spirit of God, he is astounded by the work God does to him and through him.

He was full of judgment. When the Old Testament refers to judgment, often it is speaking of justice. Micah could thunder against the injustice in the courtrooms, the injustice in the boardrooms, and the injustice in the pulpits, because the Spirit of God put in his soul a craving for righteous judgment. He understood that the God who is "no respecter of persons" (Acts 10:34) expected the same from human leadership.

He was full of might. There is a nuance between the words "power" and "might". The "might" of Micah was not so much the physical strength he needed to fight the battle, as it was the spiritual moving of God upon His work. He was looking for results only God and His authority could produce.

He was full of preaching. The natural response God's man has to God's power is a consuming passion to proclaim the message. Jeremiah put it perfectly. "His word was in mine heart as a burning fire shut up in my bones, and I was weary with forbearing, and I could not stay" (Jeremiah 20:9). By submitting to the Spirit of God, men like Jeremiah and Micah surrendered control of their lives to Him. They became mouthpieces for God.

Such a man is fearless in condemning the sins of the land. Without apology, Micah not only names the particular sins, but puts the responsibility where it belongs. Jacob has "his transgression." Israel has "his sin". Judah's brothers to the north have fallen as a result of their idols and false religion, and Micah makes them take responsibility. Rare is the preacher with the courage to name sin. Rarer still is the man with the fortitude to lay the blame at the feet of the guilty man.

America, a land poisoned by sin, is crying out for such preachers today! How the Lord must look at our land and cry, "Judgment is turned away backward, and justice standeth afar off: for truth is fallen in the street, and equity cannot enter. Yea, truth faileth; and he that departeth from evil maketh himself a prey: and the LORD saw it, and it displeased him that there was no judgment" (Isaiah 59:14-15). There is a dire need for fearless preachers and fearless preaching more concerned with God's approval than human applause.

In 1887, the English pastor Charles Spurgeon witnessed the steady compromise of the Baptist Union to which his church belonged. Liberalism was gaining a foothold in the religious world, and its effects were weakening churches on two continents. He was fond of saying, "The best way to defend a lion is to let it out of the cage." And so he did. No wonder his Bible preaching not only impacted his world, it still preaches a century later.

In the middle of the battle, Spurgeon wrote these words in his magazine:

> "The time has come for Christians to stir: The house is being robbed, its very walls are being digged down, but the good people who are in the bed are too fond of the warmth, and too much afraid of getting broken heads, to go downstairs and meet the burglars...Inspiration and speculation cannot long abide in peace. Compromise there can be none. We cannot hold the inspiration of the Word, and yet reject it; we cannot believe in the atonement and deny it; we cannot talk of the doctrine of the fall and yet talk of the evolution of spiritual life from human nature...One way or another we must go. Decision is the virtue of the hour."[20]

That is what it sounds like when a preacher is full of power. That is what it sounds like when the outlook is *"incurable"*.

CHAPTER TEN

REVIVAL HAPPENED!

IN THE COUNTRY OF IRAQ, along the Euphrates River, there is a town of 15,000 inhabitants called Al Kifl. By all appearances, the town looks normal enough for a third world country, with its bazaars, traffic, pollution, and commotion. Its claim to fame would be one of its residents reputed to be buried there, the prophet of God, Ezekiel.

To say that his ministry was 'unusual' would be a vast understatement. The visions he received from God, the commands he was to follow, and the messages he preached were unparalleled. Liberal commentators have gone so far as to say the man was crazy. One 'know it all' wrote it like this:

"Ezekiel was a true psychotic, capable of great religious insight but exhibiting a series of diagnostic characteristics: catatonia, narcissistic-masochistic conflict, schizophrenic withdrawal, delusions of grandeur and of persecution. In short, he suffered from a paranoid condition common in many great spiritual leaders."[21]

And for good measure: "D. J. Halperin attributes the extraordinary features of Ezekiels prophecy to an unconscious but overwhelming rage against females, whom he perceives as cruel and powerful, seductive and treacherous, and a more deeply buried rage against male figures because of some abuse experienced as a child."[22]

If that is what some think of the man 2600 years after his death, it is not hard to guess what his contemporaries thought.

A preacher that publicly lay on his side 430 days in a row to make a point will get a reaction. God told him to make a loaf of bread with strange ingredients, bake it over human dung, and then eat it. When Ezekiel objected, he was allowed to substitute cow dung for the human waste. Then God told him to give himself a haircut, and make three piles of the hair. He burned one pile, sliced the other with a knife, and tossed the third into the wind.

The people must have been talking, but at the end of the day, there was something they recognized. They knew there had "been a prophet among them" (Ezekiel 2:5).

So it was for Micah. We don't know the results of the revival campaign in southern Judah. Did the people repent? Did the people ignore? Did the people scoff? It may have been all of the above, but when Micah was finished, they knew a man of God had preached among them.

It is deeply discouraging to preach the Bible with a broken heart and have nothing happen. But the man of God soldiers on. Regardless of yesterday's results, today is another opportunity. If Micah's nation is truly *"incurable"*, then he cannot afford to live in pity. He must press on, and so he does, all the way to Jerusalem.

Micah 3 tells the story. We might well imagine this country preacher from the tiny village of Moresh landing at the sophisticated capital city of Jerusalem. We can almost hear the snickers and jokes. "Look at that hayseed! Where did he get those clothes? What school did he attend?" When he began to preach, they may have doubled over in laughter.

Envision a country bumpkin from the mountains of North Carolina standing on the west side of New York City, condemning opulence and arrogance. Picture a Tennessee hillbilly on the National Mall in Washington D.C., reproaching the corruption and immorality of the politicians. CNN would have a field day!

But when Micah was done, they would know a prophet was among them. He may not have looked like them, dressed like them, sounded like them, but the message was more important than the messenger.

"They lean upon the LORD, and say, Is not the LORD among us? none evil can come upon us" (Micah 3:11).

He goes right to their false security. With help from their false ministers, they had convinced themselves that God was with them. "Look at our beautiful houses! Look at our gorgeous temple! Look how much we have! God must be on our side!" Humans usually equate wealth and material items with the blessing of God.

Micah puts it all on the line. He has called them out. He has named their sin. Now, in verse 12, he proclaims their punishment:

"Therefore shall Zion for your sake be plowed as a field, and Jerusalem shall become heaps, and the mountain of the house as the high places of the forest."

He notifies them their beloved, impregnable city would be plowed down and become heaps of rubbish. The temple mount which housed their weakened religion, would become a place overgrown like a forest. As Abraham found it in Genesis 22 so it would return. The center of their hypocritical religion would face the wrath of God.

To the people of Jerusalem in Micah's day, such a message was truly powerful. There was no place more holy than the great temple built on top of Mount Zion, the very place where Abraham offered Isaac. The least holy of places would be forests, where the wild animals prowled, and death was ubiquitous. As Jerusalem was overthrown, their proud house of religion would be the stomping grounds of the lowest beasts.[23]

What a parallel in our day! Look at the buildings in America and Europe that once housed mighty preaching of the Bible, but are now empty and muted on Sunday mornings. They have died a slow, painful death, until the candle has been extinguished. *"Incurable"* indeed!

What followed was a stunning development. We don't even read the story in the book of Micah, yet, the Bible describes an extraordinary result.

Some one hundred years later, the prophet Jeremiah offended the ministerial establishment by a 'habit' he tried to lose, but found he could not. His 'habit' was to "preach the word" (2 Timothy 4:2), and when he cut loose, it usually sounded like this: "thus saith the Lord." The phrase "saith the Lord" is found an astounding 327 times in the book of Jeremiah!

When Jeremiah tried to quit preaching, the Word of God was "shut up in (his) bones" (Jeremiah 20:9) and he couldn't help himself. He had to preach, but that preaching nearly cost him his life. The ministerial elite, known as the priests and prophets, responded to the invitation with these words, "Thou shalt surely die." When they put him on trial, the man of God spoke these words in his defense: "Now amend your ways and your doings, and obey the voice of the LORD your God; and the LORD will repent him of the evil that he hath pronounced against you. As for me, behold, I am in your hand: do with me as seemeth good and meet unto you" (Jeremiah 26:8, 13-14).

It looked hopeless for Jeremiah, but God had his defense prepared. "Then said the princes and all the people unto the priests and to the prophets; This man is not worthy to die: for he hath spoken to us in the name of the LORD our God" (Jeremiah 26:16). They were followed by some elder statesmen, who told this story:

"Micah the Morasthite prophesied in the days of Hezekiah king of Judah, and spake to all the people of Judah, saying, Thus saith the LORD of hosts; Zion shall be plowed like a field, and Jerusalem shall become heaps, and the mountain of the house as the high places of a forest" (Jeremiah 26:18).

Amazing! The old country hillbilly preached in the big city, and more than 100 years later they are still quoting the message! More startling is the fact that they are quoting him accurately!

Then we stop and consider how they made it 100 years. *"Incurable"* means *"incurable"*. The example to Judah was their cousins to the North, who now belonged to the history books. When Micah preached, they were teetering on the edge of the abyss of God's judgment, yet more than ten decades later, there remained a Jerusalem, a population, and a prophet walking in the steps of Micah and Isaiah.

What happened?

The elders go on: "Did Hezekiah king of Judah and all Judah put him at all to death? did he not fear the LORD, and besought the LORD, and the LORD repented him of the evil which he had pronounced against them? Thus might we procure great evil against our souls" (Jeremiah 26:19).

Revival happened! Micah preached a powerful message on the judgment of God, and the warning came to the ears of the king. Instead of hardening his heart against God, he humbled himself and repented. His repentance led to a revival in the land, and the judgment of God was spared! God repented of the evil He planned to do!

God has a history of doing just that. Decades earlier, God repented of His promise to destroy Nineveh. A few years later, He repented of terrorizing judgments that were to fall on Israel. His pronouncements of judgment always come with a tear, with a loving desire to see true humility and sorrow for sin. When He sees that heart, nothing pleases Him more than to stop the destruction and heal the land.

It came from one man's preaching! There was no organization and there was no board. There was no fancy advertising campaign, no international ministry, and no "outside the box" thinking. It is all so simple. God said it is *"incurable"*. One country preacher with a broken heart decided he would not quit. He would keep preaching. In the little village, in the quaint town, in the growing city, and in the great metropolis, there he stands preaching until there is no more 'preach' in him.

And revival came.

No matter how dark things get, God's man must keep preaching. He must keep "abounding in the work of the Lord" (1 Corinthians 15:57). He must not become "weary in well doing" (2 Thessalonians 3:13). He must start preaching, and never stop preaching, until Jesus says, "Well done, thou good and faithful servant" (Matthew 25:21).

Five days after the outbreak of World War 1, a ship called *"Endurance"* sailed from British waters with the Antarctic as their destination. Its mission was to land on the daunting continent, and be the first humans to cross it. Twenty seven carefully chosen men, experts in diverse fields, joined the expedition's leader, Sir Ernest Henry Shackleton.

"Endurance: Shackleton's Incredible Voyage"[24] is a captivating book which tells their story. Though they failed in their original mission, the account of courage and perseverance in the face of insurmountable obstacles has left an even greater legacy. Few humans have ever experienced such hardship.

As they approached the Antarctic, their ship was frozen in place for ten months. An ice flow destroyed the hull forcing Shackleton to order them to abandon ship. For six months they lived on the frozen block eating penguins, seals, and ultimately, their dogs. When the ice flow split, they had no choice but to enter the lifeboats and head for land. The torturous, frigid conditions hammered the crew, and hope of survival diminished by the day.

Realizing there was no chance of rescue, Shackleton chose five men, and set a course for South Georgia, leaving 22 men behind at a place called Elephant Island. His 22 foot lifeboat would have to traverse 800 miles of the most dangerous waters in the world. Gale force winds of 40 mph were the norm, as were ocean swells of 20 feet. On occasion, the waves would reach as high as 52 feet and the freezing temperatures made life miserable. The smallest navigational error would mean they would miss their target, making death a certainty. Shackleton took supplies for but four weeks, realizing if they did not reach the shipping lanes in that time frame, they would be lost.

Fourteen days later, they arrived at South Georgia. For nine hours, they battled hurricane force winds until they finally landed the boat. Between them and the whaling station of Stromness lay impassable mountains. No human had ever traversed those mountains, but Shackleton had no choice. For 36 hours they staggered on, finally arriving at the station.

The 22 men left behind had long since given up hope of being rescued, but Shackleton found a way. After three desperate attempts, they were successfully evacuated, and the 28 men that had begun the journey all returned home.[25]

Hope in the midst of hopelessness. It is the reason we persevere. It is the reason we press on. When the situation is *"incurable"*, we recognize there are no human fixes, there are no human answers. But, we also understand that God can do all things.

He can even cure the *"incurable"*!

The Promise

*"Wherefore God also hath highly exalted him,
and given him a name which is above every name:
That at the name of Jesus every knee should bow,
of things in heaven, and things in earth,
and things under the earth;
And that every tongue should confess that
Jesus Christ is Lord,
to the glory of God the Father."*
(Philippians 2:9-11)

CHAPTER ELEVEN

"O LITTLE TOWN..."

A WEALTHY BUSINESSMAN was visiting missionaries in a destitute part of the world. At one particular mission, he witnessed a young woman tirelessly working with frail villagers in a medical clinic. He watched her bandage their wounds, salve their sores, dry their tears, and she did it all with a smile. In the course of conversation, he made this statement, "Madam, I would not do what you do for all the money in the world!"

She replied, "And I would not do it for all the money in the world. But, I would gladly do it for the love of Christ!"

Micah had a lot of motivations. He loved his country, and when he heard the end was near, that gave him reason to press on. He feared God, and the fact that Almighty God had brought them to the Courtroom of the Heavens to declare their fate, was more than enough to get the attention of a tenderhearted man like Micah. He was angry with a righteous anger at the compromise of the ministers, and the corruption of the leadership.

Love of country. Fear of God. Disgust with injustice. All of these are strong and healthy motivations to soldier on in the heat of battle. Yet, in the Bible, there is a motivation that exceeds all others. It is the highest impetus a man can humanly know, and it was the ultimate fuel for Micah.

Some 760 years would go by before the Apostle Paul would sum it up this way: "For the love of Christ constraineth us; because we thus judge, that if one died for all, then were all dead: And that he died for all, that they which live should not henceforth live unto themselves, but unto him which died for them, and rose again" (2 Corinthians 5:14-15).

Micah served the Lord because He loved Him. It is true his preaching was unflinching and transparent; it was loaded with warnings and condemnations that exposed the hypocrisy and corruption. But there was another side we cannot afford to miss.

Micah pointed people to Christ!

He preached about Christ their Good Shepherd. In Micah 2, the man of God castigated his people for following the House of Jacob to the north. He informed them they had made themselves enemies to God, who in turn was about to punish them as He had chastised their brothers. The ever-present reminder of the mighty Assyrian army, and their domination over their enemies, sent many a streak of panic through the nation. One did not have to be a military pundit to see they were on the fast track to bondage.

Suddenly, seemingly out of nowhere, Micah conveyed a message of hope. "I will surely assemble, O Jacob, all of thee; I will surely gather the remnant of Israel; I will put them together as the sheep of Bozrah, as the flock in the midst of their fold: they shall make great noise by reason of the multitude of men. The breaker is come up before them: they have broken up, and have passed through the gate, and are gone out by it: and their king shall pass before them, and the LORD on the head of them" (Micah 2:12-13).

That's the Good Shepherd making a promise! He would assemble them like a mighty harvest, and bring them back to the fold of Judah. Bozrah was renowned for its sheepfolds and optimal pasture lands. Better yet, He would gather them in "their fold". One day, they would be coming home.

He promised to protect a remnant. Many a time in the history of Israel, it seemed certain that Satan had finally obliterated them. His strategy through the Old Testament was to eliminate the line of Christ, and eliminate the nation of Christ. His operatives today use their violent Muslim religion to threaten the very existence of the "apple of His eye", yet they are on the losing end of that engagement. Israel is coming back with a "great noise", with a great "multitude", and with a great burst. He is the "breaker" of the barriers that have stood in their way.

"I am the good shepherd, and know my sheep, and am known of mine" (John 10:14).

He preached about Christ their King. "The LORD shall reign over them in mount Zion from henceforth, even for ever" (Micah 4:7). On the heels of the condemnation of Jerusalem in Micah three, Micah pivots 180 degrees in chapter four. His last words in chapter three left them plowed under and ruined, thinking the end is imminent, but not so! Someone is coming to rule!

The mountains of refuse that are left after God's wrath will live again. One day, "the mountain of the house of the LORD shall be established in the top of the mountains" (Micah 4:1). Those very mounds of rubble will be the destination of God's people, as they joyfully make their way up the mountain of the house of God. It will be "exalted above the hills", literally raised up so the whole world can see it. The mount where He reigns will become the focal point of the world.

What a day that will be! "Many nations" of the world will "flow" like a river to Jerusalem. Their song will be, "Come, and let us go up to the mountain of the LORD, and to the house of the God of Jacob; and he will teach us of his ways, and we will walk in his paths: for the law shall go forth of Zion, and the word of the LORD from Jerusalem" (Micah 4:2). People will want to go. People will want to learn. People will want to obey Him. The Bible will be the prominent book, and Jesus will be the preeminent Lord.

Today the name of Christ is despised. My name continually every day is blasphemed" (Isaiah 52:5). But the day will come when the mighty King will sit upon His righteous throne, the hearts of the nations will turn to Him, and the earth will finally receive her king. At last, there will be "peace, good will toward men" (Luke 2:15). "They shall beat their swords into plowshares, and their spears into pruninghooks: nation shall not lift up a sword against nation, neither shall they learn war any more" (Micah 4:3). The war colleges will close. The military will be out of business.

Micah 4:3 is written on a wall in the United Nations. What hypocrisy! An old time preacher put it like this:

> "If those boys have beaten their swords into plowshares, it only means that they have a bigger instrument with which to beat each other over the head. And if they are turning their spears into pruninghooks, they are not using them to catch fish but to gouge other nations, especially those that are weaker than they are. This verse certainly is not being fulfilled by the United Nations! They are really knocking each other out there, and there is very little agreement. It will not be fulfilled until Christ comes."[26]

With the Assyrian army rising like a mighty tide in conquering the world, there must have been many a sleepless night in Jerusalem. Yet, in the midst of their 'dangers and toils and snares', Micah prophesied of the day when "they shall sit every man under his vine and under his fig tree; and none shall make them afraid" (Micah 4:4). Vines and figs are symbols of prosperity in the Bible, so the picture shows a peaceful, prosperous, pleasant man delighting in the blessing of his King.

There is more. The Lord promised to "assemble her that halteth", to "gather her that is driven out, and her that I have afflicted" (Micah 4:6). The abused, crippled sheep of

Jerusalem that have experienced the judgment of God at the hands of men, will come home to Jerusalem, and become a "strong nation". Through the corridor of time, the Jews have witnessed the repeated destruction of the city they love, but that cycle is going to stop. The city often attacked will become the greatest of strongholds.

Micah gets to the heart of the matter. "For all people will walk every one in the name of his god, and we will walk in the name of the LORD our God for ever and ever" (Micah 1:5). Micah joins the ranks of Moses and Joshua and Elijah. "You can have a god (small 'g' god), or you can bow your knee to the LORD God. You have a choice, but it is time to decide. Who will be the king of your heart?"

That choice is available for us today. In a world ripped apart by sin and misery and trouble, we can have the joy and protection and peace of God. It is no mystery. Regardless of the choices of our leaders and ministers, an individual can seek the Lord, love the Lord, and exalt the Lord. We can choose Him as our king, and put Him on the throne of our heart.

He preached about Christ their Savior. Yet again, Micah warns them of the coming judgment. He prophesied that one day the enemy would "smite the judge of Israel with a rod upon the cheek" (Micah 5:1). The revival under Hezekiah temporarily spared the land from the wrath of God, but the dark days would return. That is the problem with revival. It only lasts as long as the people of God have tender hearts.

In 2 Kings 25 the Bible describes the events of that judgment day. Wicked King Zedekiah led the nation down the slippery slope of sin, and the Babylonian army was putting the finishing touches on Jerusalem. As Micah promised, he was smitten on the face, and his eyes were put out.

Times were desperate. Their kings failed. Their judges failed. Their businesses failed. Their prophets and priests failed. It appeared to the handful of captives being led away that Jerusalem was done for, and the royal line of David was extinguished.

Then comes the little word that changes everything - it is the hinge word of the Bible. It is the first word of Micah 5:2. *"But"*. What a word!

> "For the wages of sin is death; **but** the gift of God is eternal life through Jesus Christ our Lord" (Romans 6:23).
>
> We "were by nature the children of wrath, even as others. **But** God, who is rich in mercy, for his great love wherewith he loved us" (Ephesians 2:3-4).
>
> "He that spared not his own Son, **but** delivered him up for us all" (Romans 8:32).
>
> "The judgment was by one to condemnation, **but** the free gift is of many offences unto justification" (Romans 5:16).

Micah takes them to the most unlikely of villages, a humble town some five miles from Jerusalem. Compared to the massive buildings and gates of Jerusalem, it was an unassuming place indeed. There were "thousands" of clans and families scattered through the nation, yet, from this tiny little village, would come the One who would save the world.

He took them to the little town of Bethlehem.

"But thou, Bethlehem Ephratah, though thou be little among the thousands of Judah, yet out of thee shall he come forth unto me that is to be ruler in Israel; whose goings forth have been from of old, from everlasting" (Micah 5:2).

Hope would come from Bethlehem! Jesus, the King of all kings, the Lord of all lords, would ultimately be the ruler they had sought for. Through the corridor of time, Israel had some wonderful kings that instilled hope in the hearts of the people. From David to Solomon to Uzziah to Hezekiah, there was great optimism in the leadership, yet each one of those men proved their feet were made of clay. They could offer no permanent solutions.

But Christ would be different. He was to be the "ruler", the king with all dominion. Though He would be human (born in Bethlehem), He would also be from "everlasting". He would not be beholden to the special interests that control human leaders, but He would serve "unto" God his father.

Hope was born in that little manger in Bethlehem. We might join the prophet Micah, the escapees of Jerusalem, and multitudes of saints through the ages who have wondered if hope has run out. But that little baby in Bethlehem had something to say to the defeated Israelites, and he has a message for His people today.

Imagine you were a captive being led away in chains. Imagine your city was burning in the background, and it was your future going up in the smoke. Now listen to one of the captives open the Bible to Micah 5, and read the promises of God:

"The remnant of his brethren shall return unto the children of Israel."

"He shall stand and feed in the strength of the LORD".

"They shall abide".

"This man shall be the peace".

In Micah's day, the Assyrian army was the great threat, but the man of God reminds them that God knows how to fight the battle! He has seven shepherds and eight principal men (great leaders) at his disposal. That was a Hebrew idiom stating God has more than enough power and resources to defeat Assyria, Nimrod (Babylon), or any enemy that Satan throws at us today.

We can trust Him! We can follow Him! We can rest in Him!

God promised a "remnant". When the dust settled, they would be found to be faithful people that had persevered with patience and courage. One day, the Savior will return to this earth to establish His kingdom, and He will be looking for that remnant.

That remnant will be Israel along with those of "many people" (Micah 5:7). That remnant that once was hunted will now be the judges. Like the showers that cover the earth, they will be everywhere representing their King. The Lord will give them victory to quickly and easily defeat their foes, like "a young lion among the flocks of sheep". "All thine enemies shall be cut off", along with their strong holds, their witchcrafts, their idols, and their houses of false religion.

"And I will execute vengeance in anger and fury upon the heathen, such as they have not heard" (Micah 5:15).

James Proctor grew up in a Christian home, attending church and Sunday school in Manchester, England. In his teens, he began to read the writings a group of infidels known as *The Free Thinkers*. Gradually his faith in God was shaken, until James renounced all interest in Christianity. He joined the Free Thinkers' Society and became its president.

Some time later, James Procter became seriously ill. Fearing that he would not live, he called for a minister of the Gospel. The gentleman came to Procter's bedside and led him to Christ. With his sister by his bedside, the dying man asked her to write some lines he hoped his unbelieving friends would read. His testimony went like this:

I've tried in vain a thousand ways
My fears to quell, my hopes to raise;
But what I need, the Bible says,
Is ever, only Jesus.

My soul is night, my heart is steel,
I cannot see, I cannot feel;

For light, for life I must appeal
In simple faith to Jesus.

He died, He lives, He reigns, He pleads;
There's love in all His words and deeds;
There's all a guilty sinner needs
Forever more in Jesus.

Tho' some should sneer, and some should blame,
I'll go with all my guilt and shame;
I'll go to Him because His name,
Above all names is Jesus.[27]

That's it! From Adam to the present day, from Jerusalem to America and around the world, the answer is still the same. It is Jesus - only Jesus.

He is the answer to any *"incurable"* situation.

CHAPTER TWELVE

WOE IS ME!

AN OLD TEXAS PREACHER named John Hicks was at the doorstep of eternity. Discouragement is a powerful tool in the arsenal of the wicked one, and it is especially effective with the preachers of the Bible. John Hicks was not only at the end physically, he was also there emotionally.

A pastor named Wallace Basset did his best to comfort him in his hospital room, but was unsuccessful. He was there when the preacher spoke these dying words: "Wallace, my life is over, my preaching days are done, and I've never done anything for Jesus. I've failed, Wallace, I've failed."

Years later, Wallace Basset was meeting with the famous Southern Baptist pastor, W.A. Criswell. During the course of the conversation, Criswell related how he had been saved as a ten year old boy. When the Spirit of God was greatly convicting him, he asked permission to leave school, so that he might attend the morning service of a revival meeting. Sitting with his mother, he soaked in every word, and when the invitation was extended, the young man walked the aisle trusting Christ as Savior.

As Basset was rejoicing in the story, he asked who the evangelist was. To his amazement, Pastor Criswell told him the preacher was named John Hicks.[28]

A preacher never knows. With the word *"incurable"* ringing in his ears, there was no way Micah could ever know that King Hezekiah would hear the message, and a season of repentance would follow. He could not imagine that a century later, his message would be as alive as it was the day he delivered it, or that twenty seven centuries later, he would still be preaching.

The average church member cannot understand the battle of the preacher. It looks so simple when their pastor stands in the pulpit and speaks for forty minutes. How hard is that?

It is incredibly hard. Hours of study and work and prayer go into those forty minutes. When a preacher stands in God's pulpit, he is on the front lines of the unseen spiritual battle instigated by the "prince of the power of the air" (Ephesians 2:2). Only another preacher can commiserate when a life is poured into a message, and seemingly nothing happens.

Discouragement is the concealed struggle of preachers. They are incredibly good at putting on the smiling face in public, expertly carrying everybody else's burdens, while shouldering their own alone. They are great listeners with no one to hear them. The bouts of discouragement can be excruciating and torturous, and many a preacher tosses and turns through long, lonely nights of despair and secret turmoil.

They are neither the first, nor the only men to face such a struggle. Ask Elijah what it was like under that juniper tree, when he wanted to die. Ask David about the lonely cave of Adullam, where he was convinced that "...no man cared for my soul" (Psalm 142:4). Ask John the Baptist, trapped behind prison bars, and wondering out loud, "Art thou he that should come, or do we look for another" (Matthew 11:3)?

Micah joins the list. His nation is "incurable". The political climate, the religious compromise, the idolatry and thievery have broken Micah. The situation is hopeless and helpless, and the realization is setting in as the curse of God rests upon the land. The load is too great, and when Micah can't take it any longer, it sounds like this:

"Woe is me" (Micah 7:1)!

What a powerful word. In our English language, the word is somewhat softened. We look at someone complaining, perhaps exaggerating their troubles, and they have a 'woe is me' attitude. But there is nothing funny nor soft about this word in the Bible.

Most often, when the Bible uses the word "woe", it is followed by a prophecy of judgment upon deserving sinners. Prophets like Jeremiah, Ezekiel, Hosea, and Amos frequently began their messages with the word. The 107 times it is found in the Bible were used to get the listener's attention, and served to let them know they had a big problem.

The hardest message ever recorded may well be the words Jesus preached to the Pharisees in Matthew 23. Eight times, Jesus told them, "Woe unto you." When the seams of the world are bursting during the time of Great Tribulation, some of the most severe judgments are called the first, second, and third woe.

The word "woe" is a word of impending doom and death. When God told the wicked nations, "Woe is unto you", He was telling them they were as good as dead. When Jesus told the Pharisees, "Woe unto you", he was telling them they were as good as dead. When the woes come upon the world scene, the people are as good as dead. When Paul said, "Woe is unto me, if I preach not the gospel" (1 Corinthians 9:16), he was saying, "If I can't preach, I may as well be dead."

When Micah said, "Woe is me", he was saying he wished he were dead. He may well have spoken like John Hicks and said, "My life is over, my preaching days are done, and I've never done anything for Jesus. I've failed! I've failed!"

2700 years after the fact, we see Micah as an unqualified success. He didn't quit. He didn't compromise. Most certainly, Heaven long ago welcomed him with the words, "Well done, good and faithful servant" (Matthew 25:23). That is how we see him. That is how Heaven sees him. But that is not how he saw himself. His introspection led to very different conclusions.

I have no fruit. "I am as when they have gathered the summer fruits, as the grapegleanings of the vintage: there is no cluster to eat: my soul desired the firstripe fruit" (Micah 7:1). It is time for the summer fruit to be harvested, so Micah goes to he vineyard, yet there are no clusters there. The first ripe fruit was an early green fig, the most delicious of all, but there were none to be found. Micah cried out, "My soul desired." He desperately wanted the fruit, but the harvest had been stripped bare.

A lifetime of preaching and nothing to show for it. Eternity will reveal the multitudes of preachers that have invested their lives in a little town. They have faithfully served Christ, preached the Word, and given their very souls to the work. At the end of the day, the church is small, and the trees are bare. A lifetime of work, and like Micah, there seems to be no fruit.

Micah wished he were dead.

There are no good men. "The good man is perished out of the earth: and there is none upright among men" (Micah 7:2). With the citizens of the land exposed for their sins, Micah was left to wonder where the good men lived. He looked for a kind, benevolent man, but the leaders in the pulpits, the courtrooms, and the business centers cared nothing for others.

Micah could not find an "upright" man. No one had the courage to stand up and do right. No one had the backbone to oppose an increasingly wicked society.

He described them as lying "in wait for blood", and hunters "with a net". Some murdered a life, some murdered a reputation, but it seemed everyone was on the prowl. With "both hands" (Micah 7:3) they dove into their escapades of sin, giving their evil endeavors everything they had.

There seemed to be no honest men left. They would "wrap" up their corruption into neat packages. The "best of them" acted as a sharp brier, a thorn hedge making life difficult and impossible, when they were supposed to be a refreshing vineyard. As a result, the entire nation was in imminent danger of the wrath of God.

Micah was not done.

I cannot trust anyone. He believed he was in this all alone. In Micah 7:5, he could not trust his friends. He could not trust his guides (close friends that would give counsel and advice). He could not trust his own wife. He was forced to "keep the doors of (his) mouth from her that lieth in (his) bosom", fearing she would use his words against him. Micah's family had disintegrated in front of him. It is a desperate day when a husband/father knows that "a man's enemies are the men of his own house" (Micah 7:6).

"Woe is me." Micah has come to the place of isolation. He cannot trust his leadership, his friends, and his family, and was a lonely man. "I wish I were dead." It seems that Micah is now as *"incurable"* as his nation.

One more time, Micah is making a choice. In chapter 1, the nation's outlook was miserably bleak, but the man of God would not quit. He taught the generations of preachers to come that they have to keep pressing on, that there is no quit for a God-called preacher.

In chapter 7, his personal outlook was similarly dismal, yet once again, Micah has a lesson for God's man. This time, the pressures come from within instead of without, and are personal instead of national. His sorrows 'like sea billows roll', but Micah knows where to go, and he knows what to do.

Micah, what do you do when you are lonely? Micah, what do you do when nothing is working? Micah, what do you do when you are discouraged?

And the man of God says, "Therefore I will look unto the LORD" (Micah 7:7). The hope is not in a pill, a prescription, or a program. The hope is not in a seminar, a symposium, or a sermon. The hope is not in a psychologist, a therapist, or an analyst.

> *My hope is built on nothing less*
> *Than Jesus' blood and righteousness.*
> *I dare not trust the sweetest frame,*
> *But wholly lean on Jesus' name.*
> *On Christ the solid rock I stand,*
> *All other ground is sinking sand.*[29]

Micah runs to the Savior! *"I will look"*. He has a personal relationship with the LORD Jehovah, calling Him the "God of my salvation". In the day of discouragement, a man's walk with God will carry him.

"I will wait". The word means to wait in hope, not hopelessness. It is a confident word of resolve, leaving no doubt as to the end result. Micah was saying, "I can wait, and I will wait, because He will deliver me."

I will pray. There never was a doubt with Micah, for His walk with God was intimate. He was absolutely certain "...my God will hear me."

Micah had learned the lesson of hope, and it gave him personal victory in the war of his soul. When he was held by the bonds of discouragement and despair, his own personal example would be planted by Almighty God in His eternal words, reminding any despondent child of the King where to turn.

We look. We wait. We pray.

The personal struggle of Micah 7 becomes a prophecy for the nation of Israel. The chapter begins with the story of a hurting preacher, and closes with the story of a hurting nation. Some 137 years later, the load of sin in Jerusalem would finally bring about its collapse. The conquering Babylonians would have their day, and it would sound like this:

"Rejoice not against me, O mine enemy ... I will bear the indignation of the LORD, because I have sinned against him" (Micah 7:8-9). The enemy is gloating over the destruction of the city. Most of the inhabitants were dead (see Lamentations), and the remaining captives were taunted (see Obadiah). The appropriate word to describe Jerusalem is "darkness". Dark was the city. Dark were the gates. The last one to leave had indeed turned the lights out, and it was over.

Imagine those captives that had been carried away in chains to Babylon. Their last memories of their beloved capitol was the smoke rising to the Heavens, the bodies of the princes hanging by their necks over the city walls, the stench of the dead rotting in the streets, and the horror of women cannibalizing their own children. Now they hunker down by a little stream in a foreign country, dreading what the future would hold.

An old man pulls out a tattered parchment, which over time would come to be known as the book of Micah. He carefully lays that fragile document before the people, then points his bony finger to a promise God had given just for them. "In the day that thy walls are to be built, in that day shall the decree be far removed. In that day also he shall come even to thee from Assyria, and from the fortified cities, and from the fortress even to the river, and from sea to sea, and from mountain to mountain" (Micah 7:11-12).

The tears begin to stream down the face of that old man. He lifts up his feeble voice, and reminds the captives that it is not over! The last chapter has not yet been written! The disconsolate remnant and their posterity will have their day! "The day is coming that God will turn the lights back on in that darkened city. Better yet, He will turn on His lights in darkened hearts, and our people will see not only what their sins have wrought, but with a heart of repentance, they will turn back to Him and 'behold his righteousness'" (Micah 7:9).

The old man goes on. "Zion's enemies will be conquered. The taunters will be taunted. They mocked by asking, 'Where is your God?' Now they will plainly see our God! As they executed judgment on Israel, God will execute judgment on them. As they trod down the streets of Jerusalem, now they will be trodden down. The chickens will come home to roost!"

There is no possible way that a country preacher from Moresh could ever begin to imagine his impact. Because he allowed God to give him personal victory, he was able to encourage a captive nation. He was able to impact the grandchildren and great grandchildren of the citizens of Jerusalem, and he is still being used of God to impact people in despair.

When we are convinced that hope is gone, when we are certain there is no where to turn, when it appears that our friends have deserted us, then we know that someone has been there before. God carried his prophet through the waters. God carried his nation back to Jerusalem. God will safely carry us home.

'Mr. Anonymous' has written a lot of great poems. I like this one:

> *I passed a sandlot yesterday,*
> *Some kids were playing ball.*
> *I strolled along the third base line*
> *Within the fielder's call.*
> *"Say, what's the score?" I asked the chap.*
> *He yelled to beat the stuffin',*
> *"There's no one out, the bases full,*
> *They're forty-two to nothing!"*
> *"You're getting beat, aren't you my lad?"*
> *And then in no time flat*
> *He answered, "No, sir, not as yet we're not;*
> *Our side ain't been to bat!"*

When the circumstances seem *"incurable"*, at just the right moment, the Bible reminds us that "we ain't been to bat yet!"

CHAPTER THIRTEEN
NO ONE LIKE HE

HOPE IS A big seller. Barack Obama was elected President of the United States by offering such a promise, yet, once again, we have been reminded that a politician's slogans and actions are usually two different things. Informercials give poor people hope of becoming rich, heavy people hope of losing weight, and sick people hope of health. People want to be positive, thinking that tomorrow will be brighter and better, but so often, real life gets in the way.

Sadly, we realize there is no hope in Washington. There is no hope in Wall Street. There is no hope in the latest advancements, for no matter how successful a man may be, at the end of the day, he joins Solomon and says, "All go unto one place; all are of the dust, and all turn to dust again" (Ecclesiastes 3:20).

We have been deceived so often by our leaders that we become cynical. We watch the news thinking we have taken this journey before. We hear the promises and recognize it as a different verse of the same song. Slowly, it dawns upon us, that the mess we have created really can't be fixed.

For all our efforts, it just seems *"incurable"*.

Our national condition has found its way into the hearts and lives of people. As frail humans, we learn the hard way that we do not have the power over sins which are crushing our families, our children, our grandchildren, and our own lives. The guilt and burden is heavier than ever, and humans seek any escape they can possibly find. Some turn to the bottle. Some turn to immorality. Some turn to drugs - both legal and illegal (which are rapidly becoming legal). There has to be relief from the fear and the torment.

The hangover the next morning snaps them back to cold reality. A desperate man and a downcast woman eventually conclude their sinful condition can't be fixed. They may try religion. They may try spiritualism. But with a tattered life, they can only conclude things are *"incurable"*.

But there is an answer. The man of God from Moresh could not conclude the book of Micah without directing Israel there, and it is God's intent that we know the answer for our day:

"Who is a God like unto thee, that pardoneth iniquity, and passeth by the transgression of the remnant of his heritage? he retaineth not his anger for ever, because he delighteth in mercy. He will turn again, he will have compassion upon us; he will subdue our iniquities; and thou wilt cast all their sins into the depths of the sea" (Micah 7:18-19).

What a rhetorical question! "Who is a God like unto thee?" Israel tried Molech, Baal, and Chemosh, yet all of the false gods proved their total inability to remove the guilt of sin. Dead gods cannot give eternal life. Dead religion cannot heal a living soul. "Who is a God like unto thee?" The answer, of course, is "no one!" There is no God like Him. There never has been, and there never will be.

No one pardons like He. The word means to 'lift and carry away'. He is the one that takes the guilt and burden of our sin (our iniquities are perverse and crooked ways), lifting it off our hearts, and then removing it permanently.

No one passes by like He. This frequently used word can describe a passing over the waters, a wonderful example of God doing everything possible to save us. We have rebelled and transgressed against Him, yet He is the one that has passed over to save us. His love is beyond astounding.

No one is merciful like He. His anger, though holy and righteous, never overwhelms or overpowers Him. He delights (takes pleasure) in mercy. We may have mercy on someone out of pity, yet it is not too often we look forward to extending mercy. God is different. Extending mercy makes His day!

No one is complete like He. He forgives iniquities and transgressions and sins. No matter the description of the sin, or reason for it, He can and will forgive. The singular and the plural is used in these verses. That one sin entering a life, and the culmination of many sins destroying a life, neither is too great for His glorious mercy.

No one turns again like He. He is constantly coming back to us, pleading for repentance. How many invitations, how many offers He has given!

No one loves like He. His compassion (a maternal love that a mother would have for a child) is not a general compassion, but a personal love. It is upon us. It is upon you. It is upon me.

No one forgives like He. Sin subdues us. He subdues sin. The word subdue means that He crushes our sins under His feet, then He casts our sins into the sea. He doesn't drop them into the sea, or place them in the sea, but rather hurls them into the waters. They are not buried in the ground to be dug up again, or hidden in a deep mountain cave where they will be uncovered. They are launched to a place where they will never be found again. "God not only puts our sins out of sight (Isaiah 38:17), He also puts them out of reach (Psalm 103:12), out of mind (Jeremiah 31:34), and out of existence (Acts 3:19)."[30]

Picture the garbage man pulling up in his truck. He gathers the trash, crushes the trash, and then hauls it off to a place where it is never seen again. That is what God does with our sins.

No one is faithful like He. Ask the fathers who have gone before. He never failed them because He is truth and He is merciful. He swore to Abraham and Jacob that Israel would be multiplied, and He kept His word. We can take it to the bank. When God makes a promise, "Thou wilt perform the truth" (Micah 7:20).

"Who is a God like unto thee?" Thanks for asking!

In 1927, the songwriter, Merrill Dunlop, was crossing the Atlantic on a great ocean liner called the *Leviathan*. Walking the deck, Dunlop was mesmerized by the powerful rising of the waves. As he contemplated the mighty dimensions of the sea in its depth and breadth, his thoughts turned to Micah 7:19. "Thou wilt cast all their sins into the depths of the sea." It became personal for him, and he cried out, "My sins are blotted out, I know!"

The melody came simultaneously with the words, and a song for the ages was composed:

> *What a wondrous message in God's Word!*
> *My sins are blotted out, I know!*
> *If I trust in His redeeming blood,*
> *My sins are blotted out, I know!*
>
> *Once my heart was black, but now what joy;*
> *My sins are blotted out, I know!*
> *I have peace that nothing can destroy;*
> *My sins are blotted out, I know!*
>
> *I shall stand some day before my King;*
> *My sins are blotted out, I know!*
> *With the ransomed host I then shall sing:*
> *"My sins are blotted out, I know!"*
>
> *My sins are blotted out, I know!*
> *My sins are blotted out, I know!*
> *They are buried in the depths of the deepest sea:*
> *My sins are blotted out, I know!"*[31]

No sin is too great for His mercy. The National Oceanic Atmospheric Association claims that the deepest part of the ocean is called *"Challenger Deep"*, located in the western Pacific. It is 36,200 feet deep.[32] By contrast, Mount Everest is but 29,092 feet high.

The deepest deep is deeper than the highest high! That is home of the sins of those who have been saved. They are forever blotted out, removed, and buried in the darkest of waters. So when all hope seems to be gone, when the psychologists and the theologians and the politicians are all powerless to fix the problem, there is a cure for the incurable sinner. The cure is the blood of Jesus Christ, the Son of God, that "cleanseth us from all sin" (1 John 1:7).

An old Christian woman who had memorized much of the Bible was in failing health. A debilitating disease conquered her body, and then began to work on her mind. Though much of the Bible had once filled her heart, her memory was rapidly declining. Eventually, only one precious verse stayed with her:

"I know whom I have believed, and am persuaded that he is able to keep that which I committed unto him against that day."

By and by, part of that verse slipped its hold, and she would quietly repeat, "That which I have committed unto him." At last, as she hovered on the borderline between this world and eternity, her loved ones noticed her lips moving. When they bent down to see if she needed anything, they heard her repeating over one word of the text, "Him, Him, Him."

She had lost the whole Bible, but one word. Yet, she had the whole Bible in that one word. [33]

When it seems as if we have lost everything, that all hope is gone, and the situation seems *"incurable"*, there is one word that changes everything.

"Him."

He is the cure for the *"incurable"*!

[1] Dugard, Martin; O'Reilly, Bill (2011-09-27). Killing Lincoln: The Shocking Assassination that Changed America Forever . Macmillan. Kindle Edition.

[2] http://en.wikipedia.org/wiki/Bernard_Madoff

[3] A website documenting the staggering amount of money national and international "ministries" receive: www.ministrywatch.com. How different would America be if we returned to the primacy of the local church?

[4] Galaxie Software. (2002). 10,000 Sermon Illustrations. Biblical Studies Press.

[5] http://en.wikipedia.org/wiki List_of_federal_political_scandals_in_the_United_States

[6] http://blogs.wsj.com/law/2009/11/13/breaking-william-jefferson-gets-13-years-in-bribery-scandal/

[7] http://abcnews.go.com/Politics/rep-anthony-weiner-picture/story?id=13774605#.UI8gxrRaFek

[8] Moody, D. L. (1898). Anecdotes, Incidents, and Illustrations (51–52). Chicago; New York; Toronto: Fleming H. Revell.

[9] Waltke, B. A. Commentary on Micah. Grand Rapids, Michigan: Eerdmans Publishing Company

[10] http://ministry127.com/resources/illustration/compromise-with-a-bear

[11] Tan, P. L. (1996). Encyclopedia of 7700 Illustrations: Signs of the Times. Garland, TX: Bible Communications, Inc.

[12] http://law.justia.com/cases/oklahoma/court-of-appeals-criminal/1978/1345.html

[13] Francis L. Wellman, The Art of Cross-examination, 1903.

[14] Barker, K. L. (2001). Vol. 20: Micah, Nahum, Habakkuk, Zephaniah (electronic ed.). Logos Library System; The New American Commentary (113). Nashville: Broadman & Holman Publishers.

[15] Galaxie Software. (2002). 10,000 Sermon Illustrations. Biblical Studies Press.

[16] Lister, Mosie. How Long Has It Been. 1956.

[17] Osbeck, K. W. (1996). Amazing grace: 366 inspiring hymn stories for daily devotions (51). Grand Rapids, MI: Kregel Publications.

[18] http://en.wikipedia.org/wiki/Code_of_the_Secret_Service

[19] Beyer, Rick. The Greatest Presidential Stories Never Told. New York; Harper Publishing

[20] Iain Murray, The Forgotten Spurgeon, p. 143. Carlisle, Pennsylvania: Banner of Truth

[21] Broome, E.C., Ezekiels Abnormal Personality, JBL 65 (1946) 277–92.

[22] Block, Daniel I., NICOT: The Book of Ezekiel, Chapters 1-24. Eerdman's Publishing Company.

[23] Waltke, B. A Commentary on Micah. Grand Rapids, Michigan: Eerdmans Publishing Company

[24] Lansing, Alfred (2008-03-03). Endurance: Shackleton's Incredible Voyage. New York: Perseus Books Group. Kindle Edition.

[25] http://www.shackletonfoundation.org/index.php/sir-ernest-shackleton/endurance-1914-16

[26] McGee, J. V. (1991). Vol. 29: Thru the Bible commentary: The Prophets (Jonah/Micah) (electronic ed.). Thru the Bible commentary (121). Nashville: Thomas Nelson.

[27] Osbeck, K. W. (1996). Amazing grace: 366 inspiring hymn stories for daily devotions (189). Grand Rapids, MI: Kregel Publications.

[28] Morgan, R. J. (2000). Nelson's complete book of stories, illustrations, and quotes (electronic ed.) (226–227). Nashville: Thomas Nelson Publishers.

[29] Mote, Edward. "My Hope is Built." Mote's Hymns of Praise, 1836.

[30] Barker, K. L. (2001). Vol. 20: Micah, Nahum, Habakkuk, Zephaniah (electronic ed.). Logos Library System; The New American Commentary (135). Nashville: Broadman & Holman Publishers.

[31] Osbeck, K. W. (1996). Amazing grace: 366 inspiring hymn stories for daily devotions (194). Grand Rapids, MI: Kregel Publications.

[32] http://oceanservice.noaa.gov/facts/oceandepth.html

[33] Tan, P. L. (1996). Encyclopedia of 7700 Illustrations: Signs of the Times. Garland, TX: Bible Communications, Inc.

Made in the USA
San Bernardino, CA
24 October 2013